D0065973

Ron Bowman

THE BIBLICAL PRINCIPLES OF DISCIPLESHIP

THE BIBLICAL PRINCIPLES OF DISCIPLESHIP

Foreword by Robert E. Coleman

ALLAN COPPEDGE

FRANCIS ASBURY PRESS
of Zondervan Publishing House
Grand Rapids. Michigan

The Biblical Principles of Discipleship
Copyright © 1989 by Allan Coppedge

Francis Asbury Press is an imprint of Zondervan Publishing House,
1415 Lake Drive, S.E., Grand Rapids, Michigan 49506.

Library of Congress Cataloging-in-Publication Data

Coppedge, Allan.
    The Biblical Principles of Discipleship / Allan Coppedge.
        p.   cm.
    Bibliography: p.
    Includes index.
    ISBN 0-310-75350-3
    1. Christian life—Biblical teaching. I. Title.
BS680.C47C67   1988
248.4–dc19   88-7749
                                              CIP

Most Scripture quotations are from the Revised Standard Version. In some instances
the author has made his own translation.

All rights reserved. No part of this publication may be reproduced, stored in a
retrieval system, or transmitted in any form or by any means—electronic,
mechanical, photocopy, recording, or any other—except for brief quotations in
printed reviews, without the prior permission of the publisher.

Edited by Harold W. Burgess and Robert D. Wood

Printed in the United States of America

90 91 92 93 / BC / 10 9 8 7 6 5 4 3 2

To the very special people of
The Barnabas Foundation
who share with me a vision
for being and making disciples of Jesus

contents

fOREWORD

God is making a people for His glory. In this divine purpose of creation and redemption lies the mandate to disciple all nations.

The word disciple means learner, as in the sense of an apprentice. By definition, then, disciples of Christ follow Him, and in so doing grow into His likeness. Herein is the essence of His plan to reach the world with the gospel. For as learners mature in the character of Jesus, they inevitably become involved in His ministry of discipleship; and as their disciples repeat the process, through multiplication the nations will come to know Him whom to know aright is life everlasting.

Our Lord's Great Commission brings this strategy into climactic focus. There is nothing new about it. The command simply enunciates what Christ had already demonstrated. Nor is the commission a special call to service for a few full-time workers; it is a way of life bequeathed to the whole body of believers—the way Christ directed His life while He ministered among us in the flesh, and now the lifestyle He expects His disciples to emulate.

Allan Coppedge lifts up the basic content of this new life as seen in the unfolding drama of salvation. With keen insight he observes the ever-present objective of discipleship, not just in the teaching of Christ, but in the initiative of God throughout the Scriptures.

What makes the story especially meaningful to me is the author's own commitment to disciplemaking. I have known Dr. Coppedge for a long time, first as a student and then as a colleague; and it is an inspiration to see how he seeks to practice the principles he teaches. Over the years I have watched him gather a small group of young men and lead them in a vigorous discipline of spiritual formation. An enlarging contingent of these men has gone forth with renewed vision and dedication to disciple others, and the end is not yet.

Only when teaching becomes incarnate in flesh and blood does it become convincing. That is why it is such a joy to commend this volume to you. The author has earned the right to be heard. He writes from a perspective of extensive study in the field, to be sure. But more than that, he speaks from personal experience, and in this he sets before us a proved pattern of biblical discipleship.

Robert E. Coleman

preface

Discipleship is based on personal relationships. I am deeply grateful to the Lord for the special people He has brought into my life both to help me be a disciple of Jesus and to help me learn the process of making disciples. Several have had a particularly influential role in my life in this regard. To Dr. Robert Coleman I am indebted for sharing with me the vision of discipleship after Jesus' pattern. I am deeply appreciative of the formative influences that Dr. Coleman and Dr. Dennis Kinlaw have had upon my growth, first as a student and subsequently as a disciplemaker. I am also grateful for Ray Hundley's impact upon my life. We went to the mission field together in the early 1970s, where we first began deliberate attempts at making disciples. Ray's influence on me and in my understanding of discipleship has been very marked.

Since I came to teach at Asbury Theological Seminary in 1977, a number of men and women have expressed a desire to be a part of some intentional discipleship training. Beginning with one group of men, a sizeable network of groups has develped at the seminary and at Asbury College. Several local churches have likewise asked for help to establish similar discipleship groups within their congregations. Further, some mission organizations have asked for assistance to do the same kind of discipleship training with their personnel overseas. To coordinate these activities of discipleship training, The Barnabas Fondation, Inc., was established in 1980. The Foundation continues to serve in the encouragement, promotion, and direction of discipleship training, with a special focus on preparation of spiritual leadership in the basic biblical principles of the discipleship method.

One of the activities of the Barnabas Foundation for the last several years has been an orientation retreat twice a year for those involved in discipleship groups. The purpose of the retreats has been to provide a biblical and theological foundation for the actual practice of discipleship in everyday living. The studies presented in this book grew of of those retreats. Since other leaders and disciplemakers have asked for this material, I have attempted to set it down in this form. It is not designed as a manual on how to do discipleship; rather, the intent is to provide the underlying scriptural foundation upon which the practice of discipleship is built. The Barnabas Foundation has seen these concepts serve effectively as the basis for a wide range of groups which are involved in everyday discipleship training. It should not surprise us that if principles are biblical, they work in practical experience.

I am deeply indebted to those on The Barnabas Foundation staff who have helped shape this material. I am especially grateful to Paul Law for his valuable assistance in hammering out the basic content of this material for our retreats. His contribution both to these concepts and to the ministry of the Foundation cannot be overstated. A special word of thanks must also go to David Cosby, Stuart Palmer, and Bill Ury for their assistance in refining and reshaping the studies in this book.

A word of thanks must also go to those who have read the manuscript and made significant suggestions for its final form. In this regard, I am grateful to Mr. John Dendiu and to Dr. Matt and Mary Friedeman. I especially appreciate the many hours of assistance given by Dr. Richard Sherry and Dr. Harold Burgess in revising the manuscript. All the shortcomings that remain are entirely my own responsibility. I am also thankful to the office staff of The Barnabas Foundation that made the production of this book possible. Finally, I am particularly grateful to the Lord for those people who have been a part of The Barnabas Foundation and who have inspired me in the ministry of making disciples for Jesus. My gratitude to them is inestimable.

Allan Coppedge
The Barnabas Foundation
Asbury Theological Seminary
Wilmore, Kentucky 40390

introduction

Today's rising interest in discipleship grows out of the experience of the evangelical church as it discovers it can no longer exist just to do evangelism and provide worship for believers. While the church is probably seeing as many decisions for Christ as it ever has in its history, it is not the strong, virile force it ought to be in changing the world for God. Rather, as Paul warned might happen (Rom. 12:2), the church seems to have allowed the world to be the change agent. Accordingly, many who do become Christians soon grow cold; others seem to fall entirely away from their commitment to Christ. The experience of the church demonstrates that something more than outreach is essential for its survival, if for nothing else.

At the same time that the church feels a lack within its own experience, it is learning increasingly to measure itself against the Word of God. This in turn has led to the discovery that the church is not the vibrant power for God that the New Testament church was. In particular, it finds that it is filled with a disproportionate number of "babes in Christ." Relatively few young men/young women or fathers/mothers grow to maturity in the faith (1 John 2:12–14). Obviously, something more than perfunctory follow-up must be done if new believers are going to become like the vital Christians of the New Testament.

As the church searches the Scriptures for answers to remedy its weakness, it recognizes that the discipleship process is a key to God's plan both to strengthen the church and to reach the world by raising up a group of men and women who reflect His own character. When Jesus came to fulfill God's purposes in the world, one of His key methods was disciplemaking. The church is trying again to come to grips with the meaning and power of this process, and to take it as seriously as Jesus planned.

In response to this rediscovery of Jesus' method of making disciples, a sizeable body of literature has appeared. Some use the word *discipleship* in the broadest possible way, meaning any aspect of care for Christians that comes after evangelism. Thus we have, for example, denominational boards of discipleship. Discipleship is also used to describe almost every phase of Christian education. But *discipleship* is properly employed more specifically when it refers to the methodology Jesus used to train the Twelve. It is toward this more definite focus that a number of books have appeared in recent years. Most have some reference to Jesus' patterns, but their chief concern is implementation. Such books, aimed at doing something practical in response to the church's need, come as a helpful contribution by insisting on the present application of this key New Testament process.

Receiving significantly less attention are the biblical and theological principles underlying the discipleship process. This biblical/theological dimension is concerned with the deeper purposes for which discipleship is designed, not just with the practical mechanics of disciplemaking. Such a perspective, examining God's entire plan and purpose as well as His revealed means for accomplishing it, must often ask "why?"

Not a great many authors have given *significant* attention to the underlying biblical and theological principles of discipleship. One older work is A. B. Bruce's *The Training of the Twelve*. Unfortunately, Bruce wrote at the end of the nineteenth century, and his study is not so helpful as it once was since he does not address specific needs of the contemporary church. He discusses a number of Jesus' teachings with little direct reference either to the process of discipleship or its goals. From the perspective we are taking here, this limits the book's usefulness. By far the best modern work in this area is Robert E. Coleman's *The Master Plan of Evangelism*. In this contemporary classic, Coleman analyzes Jesus' strategy for training His disciples and identifies basic principles of the discipleship process. Building on this foundation, he produced a more recent book entitled *The Master Plan of Discipleship*. This latter work, in essence a study of Acts, explores ways Jesus' method was implemented in the early church.

The purpose of this present study is to look at the larger biblical and theological framework that surrounds discipleship. Of necessity, we will also examine certain specific methods that are a part of that process. The book grew out of a conviction that discipleship, properly understood, must be seen within the larger context of God's purposes. Discipleship is a means, not merely an end in itself. It is essential for the church to understand what these means were designed to produce. What are God's purposes and how are these objectives spelled out in His Word? Once we understand what God is after, it will be possible to see the process of discipleship in its rightful place.

One of the major concerns from our perspective is that so many books on discipleship seem to imply that its primary (and perhaps only) purpose is evangelism. The church must understand that God's objectives are far broader than outreach. All that Christians do should be designed to glorify God, and the Lord has made it clear that certain specific things glorify Him. Three that bring special glory are 1) a growing relationship between believers and God, 2) development of Christlikeness in character, and 3) fruitful service for the Lord.

Regarding service for God, the holy Scriptures teach that believers have a twofold responsibility for ministry. The first area of responsibility is the building up of the body of Christ, and the other is outreach to the world. One of the ways in which Christians touch the world is through evangelism, but it is not the only one. This means that evangelism is a significant part of God's objectives, but only one part of one's total service for God. At the same time, service for God is only a sample of the several ways in which God is glorified by those who belong to Him. Accordingly, one of the purposes of this book is to address the larger issue of God's objectives for His people and then to see how the process of discipleship serves as a means to accomplish God's ends.

We cannot adequately understand God's purposes for mankind if our range of information is limited to the New Testament. The New Testament makes it clear that Jesus and the early church understood that His appearance and ministry were the fulfillment of God's plan that He gradually unfolded over many centuries. Thus we must first consider the Old Testament in our investigation. The structural relationship between the Old and New Testaments is that of promise and fulfillment. Thus there is no understanding of what is happening in the New Testament without significant appreciation for what God did in the Old Testament. It is particularly important to identify what God was after when He established a people for Himself at Sinai. At that crucial point in Israel's history, God made known what He wants. He described the people who were to be His and began to reveal the process by which they were to become that people.

Accordingly, in this study chapter 1 takes us back to the time of the Exodus when God began to spell out His objectives for those who belonged to Him. Chapter 2 examines ways Jesus used to establish the New Covenant, with some significant parallels to the Old. Jesus regarded His own ministry as a fulfillment and expansion of God's original purposes. Jesus' method of discipleship is introduced here as a part of implementing those larger designs. Chapter 3 explores qualifications essential in potential disciples of Jesus, and this is followed in chapter 4 by a description of the chief components of the discipleship method.

Chapter 5 analyzes the training of the disciples, along with strategy for using them to reach the entire world. The kind of servant-disciples Jesus wants to produce is described in chapter 6, while chapter 7 discusses Jesus' commissioning of the Twelve to their life work of making other disciples. Chapter 8 explores the need for the Holy Spirit's fullness for those who would be and make disciples. The Great Commission and its first fulfillment is the heart of chapter 9. Chapter 10 discusses the ongoing process of disciplemaking through an illustration of one man trained by the apostles. Barnabas' example focuses on the way the discipleship process multiplied in the life of the early church. Finally, the last chapter reviews key biblical principles in their relationship to God the Father, God the Son, and God the Holy Spirit. Thus the book closes with a trinitarian summary of the basic biblical principles of discipleship.

By beginning with the Old Testament and then working through the New Testament, we will get a perspective on the purposes of God that run throughout the Bible. It is a proper task of Christian theology to collect and synthesize as much biblical data as possible. It will not do to isolate a single passage, a single book, or even a single Testament. The whole Bible is the Word of God and must be taken seriously in our effort to understand what God has done in the world and what He wants us to do. This book is particularly concerned with examining how discipleship is for God's glory. Therefore, we cannot escape the responsibility of discovering more adequately who God is and what He wants us to be and do.

1

Becoming the people of God

A basic premise of this book is that the New Testament concept of discipleship is nourished by theological roots in the Old Testament. These are most clearly seen in the book of Exodus. Exodus in turn is dependent upon Genesis, which focuses on God's personal relationship with six men and their families: Adam, Noah, Abraham, Isaac, Jacob, and Joseph. Genesis establishes the truth for all the rest of Scripture that God desires a personal relationship with individuals. Only with that firmly settled in our minds is it possible to move on to Exodus. Here we have the story of Israel's establishment as the people of God and the formation of a nation. More than that, Exodus shows us how individuals relate to God and to others who belong to Him. Exodus, then, offers us more than an early history of the people who later became the Jewish nation; it reveals the essential principles for those who desire to be God's people today. This, as I have already suggested, is especially important in relation to the New Testament concept of discipleship. Discipleship, as the term is employed here, can begin only in a personal relationship with the Lord and with a desire to be formed as one of "His people."

THE CONTEXT: THE EXODUS

Exodus is the story of a people in covenant relationship with God. The high point, the heart of the book, is the description of the establishment of this covenant between God and Israel at Sinai (chaps. 19–24). Yet God's relationship to Israel and the establishment of the covenant began long before. To understand their becoming the covenant people of God we must know something of the pattern of God's earlier workings with Israel. Genesis provides this important background information.

Exodus presupposes that its readers are acquainted with the history of the human race in general and of the Jews in particular. The account also assumes an awareness of the creation of man and of the entrance of sin into the world as well as the early general history recorded in Genesis 1–11. Further, it presumes a knowledge of God's attempt to rectify the problem of sin introduced in Genesis by means of the covenant relationship with Abraham and his descendants (Gen. 12–50). God entered into a covenant with Abraham and his descendants and their families in turn. The story of those covenant relationships sets the stage for the opening of Exodus.

So God's relationship with Israel began long before their cry to Him for deliverance from the threat of destruction as a nation (Ex. 2). Through their acquaintance with the Genesis story, the Israelites already knew something of the God on whom they called. They knew that He had great power and, more particularly, that He had entered into special relationships with people who belonged to Him. This revelation of Himself, carried by oral tradition, is implicit in the cry of the Hebrews to God.

THE BASIS: REDEMPTION BY GRACE

The first twelve chapters of Exodus provide both a historical and a symbolic picture of God's redemption of His people. The problem is introduced in chapter 1. The threat on the lives of all male Hebrew children means in effect a threat to national existence. Already enslaved, they now face destruction as a people. Yet the seriousness of physical threats must not overshadow the second part of the problem which is a danger to their spiritual welfare. In bondage they are not free to be the people of God, to serve Him, or to follow where He leads. Further at issue is the fulfillment of God's promises to the patriarchs. Is God powerful enough to do what He promises? Is He a God of truth who does what He says? Thus Israel has a spiritual problem as well as a physical problem at the story's outset.

The solution begins with the call of Moses (Ex. 2–4). God's answer is initiated with the choice of a mediator who bears His word to Israel and helps to bind the Hebrews to Him. Through the mediator God reveals His mighty power to redeem the nation (Ex. 5–12). By supernatural intervention in the plagues, God demonstrates His transcendent power over all the gods of Egypt, physically freeing His people from slavery and the threat of death. Further, He sets them free spiritually to be His people and to follow His leading for their lives.

The climax of God's physical deliverance comes in Exodus 12 with the story of the Passover. Here God provides a solution to the threat of death by bringing judgment upon all the land. His deliverance includes a number of key theological principles: 1) God's willingness to accept a substitute for another's life, 2) the blood of a lamb shed as a symbol of life given up for life, 3) the sacrificial meal as a symbol of fellowship between God and His people, and 4) the redemption of God's people from their state of slavery and bondage. Each of these demonstrates a basic way in which God works. All of them reappear throughout Israel's history and eventually find complete expression in the Cross of Christ.

Thus, it is evident that the first key element in becoming the people of God is deliverance by His grace. This historical perspective in Exodus provides all future generations with a summary of the principles by which God works to establish a people for Himself. All are under the spiritual threat of slavery to sin, eternal death, and their inability to serve God or follow His leading. God's solution to human problems begins with a mediator who bears His word to people and leads them to Himself. This mediator is also the one by whom God supernaturally works the miracle of His redemption, making it possible for His people to be free to belong to Him fully. Throughout the rest of Scripture the Exodus events serve as object lessons for the revelation of God's truth to His people. They demonstrate the basic ways in which God works through relationships with His own.

In the New Testament it is Jesus who fulfills the role of Mediator, bearing the Word of God to men and bringing them into fellowship with Him. Part of that mediating role comes with the Cross, which can be understood only against the backdrop of the Passover of Exodus 12. Jesus without sin is the perfect sacrifice who substitutes His life for others like the lamb without blemish. His blood shed on the cross is His life poured out in death so that judgment and death might not come upon those who look to Him. By means of His substitutionary death, a supernatural spiritual deliverance is made available to all. On that basis they can be freed from the slavery of sin and redeemed by God's grace to become His people. Thus, both Testaments show that the first step toward becoming the people of God is redemption by God's grace.

THE BLESSING: PROVISION FOR NEEDS

The second part of becoming a people of God pertains to God's blessings and provision for those He has redeemed. Exodus 13–18 gives us a graphic portrayal of what God does for those whom He has delivered. Powerful enough to set His people free, He is good enough to meet their needs. Initially, He supplies guidance in the pillar of cloud by day and the pillar of fire by night (Ex. 13). Later He intervenes to protect His people from Pharaoh's armies that seek to reenslave them (Ex. 14). Then come the occasions of God's meeting the physical needs of His people, water (Ex. 15, 17) and food in the form of manna and quail (Ex. 16). These are followed by an example of God's ability to protect His people from hostile forces when He supported Joshua in fighting off the Amalekites (Ex. 17). Finally, God gives wisdom and guidance for the administration of a new nation through Jethro's advice to Moses when the latter needed assistance to establish his priorities. Jethro counsels him about multiplying himself effectively to do God's work (Ex. 18).

Each part of the story of God's provision (Ex. 13–18) finds a parallel in the life of every believer. God expresses His careful concern for those who belong to Him by 1) providing guidance for them, 2) protecting them from backsliding and again falling prey to the forces of evil, 3) providing for their basic physical needs, 4) assisting in spiritual battles with the forces of evil, and 5) providing counsel and wisdom from others about their life priorities and how to multiply themselves effectively for ministry.

LIVING AS THE PEOPLE OF GOD: BASIS IN COVENANT RELATIONSHIP

When the offer of the covenant comes (Ex. 19–24), it is made to a people who know both the redeeming grace of God and the desire and ability of God to provide for His own. That is why God begins by saying, "You have seen what I did to the Egyptians and how I bore you on eagles' wings and brought you to myself" (Ex. 19:4). God's offer is based upon what Israel has already seen God do. They know something of His power and His goodness. They have seen Him deliver from danger and have experienced His provisions in time of want. Their own experience provides a basis for them to trust God in this deeper way and to enter into a more significant relationship with Him. God, accordingly, confronts Israel at Sinai and challenges the Israelites to become a people of His "own possession among all peoples" (Ex. 19:5). He calls them to a unique and special relationship that will require a deeper covenant commitment from them.

Some scholars have noted that this covenant resembles treaties of the ancient Near East where an emperor or overlord makes a binding agreement with a vassal. Yet God's covenant is far more personal than such suzerainty treaties. In it God offers to enter into a deep personal relationship with Israel in a unique and ongoing way.

Israel must respond to God's offer, choosing whether to continue with Him or to draw back. Their decision is based on their choice to trust Him in a way that they have not yet experienced. They had practiced some degree of trust when God led them out of Egypt and had known further growth in their relationship with Him during the intervening three months of their journey from Egypt to Sinai. Now, based on a growing awareness of who God is and what He is like, they are invited to a deeper level of confidence in Him by committing themselves to Him in a covenant relationship. At the bottom line, as it usually is in Scripture, God's people are called to live by faith.

A covenant commitment, then, is for those whom God has redeemed by grace and who have experienced His provision for their lives. It is a deeper relationship with the God who has redeemed and provided, and it will involve a commitment to Him based upon a greater measure of faith than previously experienced. God is not content solely with the redemption of His people and the meeting of their needs. He wants a more intimate relationship with them. The call of Jesus to a handful of followers to become His disciples closely parallels this deeper covenant relationship. The response of the Twelve is based upon a previous experience of God's grace in repentance and their initial faith in Jesus.

THE OBJECTIVES OF THE COVENANT: GROWING RELATIONSHIP WITH GOD

God's introduction of the covenant is made in Exodus 19:5–6. "Now therefore, if you will obey My voice and keep My covenant, you shall be My own possession among all peoples; for all the earth is mine, and you shall be to Me a kingdom of priests and a holy nation." God's invitation to be His own possession signals His desire for a closer, more intimate, personal relationship with His people, an invitation which always comes to those who have begun to follow Him.

Both Testaments show that God desires this personal relationship with individuals as well as with the group that makes up the nation. Some scholars prefer to view the establishment of a covenant at Sinai as a purely national event that involves no individual relationship with God. This is a serious misunderstanding of the biblical picture. At Sinai, God addresses individuals who together are starting to follow Him. He speaks also to the nation, of course. This is the reason that establishment of the covenant with the nation of Israel in Exodus follows the picture of God's personal relationship with individuals and their families in the book of Genesis. The entire book of Exodus presupposes a theological understanding of a God who enters into personal relationships with human beings. Exodus then moves on to show that those individuals *together* may covenant with God.

When God describes the people who are to be His own possession and who desire to grow in their relationship with Him, He indicates that He is looking for two major characteristics. He describes His people as 1) a "kingdom of priests" and 2) a "holy nation" (Ex. 19:6), demonstrating, respectively, God's concern for ministry and character. Because of their centrality from God's point of view, these goals must become life objectives in a significant sense for everyone who desires to be a part of His people, whether under the old or the new covenant.

THE OBJECTIVES OF THE COVENANT: SERVICE FOR GOD

God's desire for a kingdom of priests is related to His concern that everyone who belongs to Him must minister in some way on His behalf. Understanding the kind of priestly service in which God is interested is impossible without an appreciation of the role of a priest in the Old Testament. Fortunately, the immediate context in Exodus provides the necessary information about some of the major functions of a priest. In Exodus 18 when Jethro advises Moses concerning his leadership of the people of God, he mentions two of the major priestly responsibilities. One is to "teach them the statutes and decisions and make them know the way in which they must walk and what they must do" (Ex. 18:20). Moses is to spend time with God, know God's Word, and be able to communicate it to God's people. Out of his own intimacy with the Lord he is to understand what God says and then be His vehicle for communicating His Word to others.

The other side of priestly responsiblity was that Moses was to "represent the people before God, and bring their cases to God" (18:19). Priests are to spend time with people and help them come into the presence of God. They are to involve themselves with people and help them learn to seek His forgiveness, offer sacrifices, learn to worship, and live with the God who redeemed them. So the priestly task was twofold. Priests were first to spend time with God and bear God's word to men. Second, they were to spend time with men and bring them into right relationship with God. Priests serve, then, as mediators between God and men.

It is this role God describes when He seeks a people who are to be a kingdom of priests for Him. Israel, individually and collectively, was to spend time with God and know His word so that they might teach and communicate His will to the world. They were to bear God's revelation and to communicate the oracles of God to others. Further, they were to help other individuals and nations come into the presence of God, learn to seek His forgiveness, and know how to worship and live in a right relationship with Him. In other words, they were to serve as mediators between God and men.

A proper understanding of this priestly role carries enormous significance with regard to God's reason in the Old Testament for choosing one nation over others. He did not, as some allege, play favorites or neglect other nations. He chose Israel for a ministry responsibility precisely because He is concerned about the whole world. That is why He looks for a people of His own possession "among all peoples." In the midst of His offer to Israel He reminds them that "all the earth is [His]" (Ex. 19:5). Here God speaks out of His concern to reach all the earth. Israel is to be His vehicle for that purpose.

The election of Israel, then, does not refer to an absolute, unconditional, personal salvation for each member of the nation. It is an appointment to responsibility for a priestly ministry to other nations. It is, therefore, an election to a ministry assigned to those who belong to the Lord. A proper understanding of the concept of election at Sinai will be of immense value in understanding other passages dealing with election throughout the Scriptures. Rather than choosing a select few for saving grace and abandoning others, God chooses people for His service because He is concerned about the entire world.

The covenant offer to Israel has clear implications for evangelism, discipleship, and missions. God has an important purpose for those who belong to Him. Particularly, that includes proclaiming God's Word and bringing other people to a right relationship with Him. For those who seek a deeper covenant relationship with God, as the discipleship process signifies, the implicit commitment is to minister to others. This ministry will emphasize communication of the Word of God and helping people come to God and live in His presence.

THE OBJECTIVES OF THE COVENANT: HOLINESS OF CHARACTER

Becoming a holy nation is another aspect of being a part of the people of God. While a "kingdom of priests" concerns service for God, the "holy nation" aspect of the covenant has to do with character. God is concerned with what people *do,* but He is more concerned about what they *are.*

When God chooses Israel to be a holy nation, He emphasizes that He wants them to be holy because He intends that they will be like Himself. His emphatic exhortation is, "Be holy, for I am holy" (Lev. 11:44–45). Throughout Leviticus God repeatedly describes Himself as holy, communicating in many of these passages His desire that His people participate in this holiness of character.

The centrality of God's holiness is illustrated in the relationship of His name to the concept of the holy. In Exodus 3:14 God reveals His name to Moses, "I AM WHO I AM." From that point He repeatedly underlines the importance of what He has to say with the formula "I am the Lord" (Ex. 6:2, 7–8, etc.). The first time an adjective is attached to "I AM" is in Leviticus 11:44–45 where He says, "I am holy." Holiness is the very essence of what God is. His nature, represented by His name, is holy. Though many other qualities are characteristic of God, at the heart of them all is His holiness.

Further confirmation of this appears throughout Scripture. For example, Isaiah sees the Lord as King sitting high upon His throne and seraphim around the King crying to one another, "Holy, holy, holy is the Lord God of hosts" (Isa. 6:3). Can we doubt that this revelation of the holiness of His character gave the prophet a model for his designation of God as "the Holy One of Israel"?

God makes clear to His people that His character is unchanged in the light of further revelation, for an almost identical vision is given at the end of the New Testament in Revelation 4. Here the four living creatures never cease to sing around the throne of God, "Holy, holy, holy is the Lord God Almighty, who was and is and is to come!" (Rev. 4:8). It is evident that this is what God's character *was* like, *is* like, and is *going to be* like. His basic nature does not change, and it is holy. While many other adjectives become attached to God's person throughout Scripture, they all must be understood in the light of His holiness. Though He is righteous, loving, and merciful, it is a holy righteousness, a holy love, a holy mercy. It is His holiness that conditions His other attributes.

When God tells a people that He wants them to be holy, He is saying in effect that they are to be like Him. They obviously cannot be like Him in His supernatural attributes, but His desire is that they reflect His moral character. It is in this context, i.e., a description of Israel's moral character, that God begins to elaborate in Exodus 20 what it means for Him to call them to be a holy nation.

He made mankind in His own image and likeness (Gen. 1:26–27), including His moral image. This moral image centered on His holiness and was expressed in righteousness and love. The moral image of God was marred with the entrance of sin into the world (Gen. 3), and it is part of His purpose in entering into covenant relationships with us to restore in us that original image of Himself. The covenant relationship God established with the patriarchs, and now in Exodus with Israel, was not only to yield a new and deeper relationship with Himself, it was also to begin transforming individuals into a reflection of His own image and likeness. Thus God's concern has to do with relationships and with character. He wants men to be rightly related to Him, but He wants them to be like Him in their basic nature as well.

So any proper understanding of the essential objectives of the people of God must not only include service for Him as priests to others, but must also include holiness of character because He is holy. For all those, then, who desire to enter into covenant relationships with the Lord, especially in a discipleship relationship, these two objectives must assume a primary place. God's people are to be concerned about their service for Him and about their character as a reflection of His nature.

THE RELATIONSHIP OF SERVICE
TO CHARACTER

Service and character are closely related. God's objective for His people to reach all the nations of the earth cannot be fulfilled adequately unless His people are holy as He Himself is holy. It is significant that the gods of a nation are often identified with the character of the nation itself. So when we look at the Romans and find that they are severe, stoic, distant, and unapproachable, it is not surprising to discover that their gods are the same. The Canaanites, in turn, were licentious, loose living, immoral; and their gods exhibited the same characteristics. God's plan is that when others look at Israel they will see something of His own character. He wants His people to be holy so that in their role as His representatives to the rest of the world, they will show forth His character and nature. To the degree that Israel was holy they would be able effectively to carry out their missionary responsibility to bear God's Word to others and bring them into a right relationship with Him. To the extent that they were unholy, they would fail (cf. Ezekiel 36).

The link between service and character also has another dimension. If one is close enough to God to be made like His character, then the things that touch God's heart will also be on the hearts of His people. One of the foremost of His concerns is the peoples of all the earth. He desires that all men know Him and enter into a relationship with Him. If Israel becomes like God in their nature, they will carry a burden for all people. It is interesting to observe throughout the Old Testament that those most intimate with God and most reflective of His nature are those who are most often responsbile for calling Israel to fulfill its evangelistic mission in the world.

From the beginning, then, God looked for holy servants, those willing to do His will fully and minister for Him in the world. Such people would be reflective of God's own holy nature. Exodus shows that from the beginning of the nation God revealed that these two elements are essential for a people who are truly His. These continued to be central throughout the Old and New Testaments. They are central today.

THE MEANS TO ACCOMPLISH GOD'S OBJECTIVES: LIVING UNDER AUTHORITY

In Exodus when God offers to enter into a covenant commitment with Israel, He not only sets forth His objectives, He begins to spell out the means to accomplish them. The first of these means is *learning to live under the authority of*

God. This is related to His desire for a people who will be a *kingdom* of priests. A kingdom did not refer to a geographical area at this early stage of Israel's life but to God's kingly rule over His people. Further exploration of God's revelation at Sinai reveals that this is just what God was after. He was creating a theocracy (government by the immediate direction of God) over which He Himself would rule as the Sovereign of the nation.

Hundreds of years later, when Israel insists on a human king, Samuel struggles before the Lord over the matter. The Lord tells him to give Israel a king because the people rejected not Samuel but the Lord as King (1 Sam. 8:7). Yet even in this limited monarchy, the king represents God who is still the ultimate Sovereign. Israel's king is never to act purely on his own authority, but is always under the authority and direction of God.

The picture of God as ruling King runs through Scripture to the very end of the book of Revelation. Kingship is a concept that centers primarily on the question of authority. God indicates that those who enter into a covenant commitment with Him must be willing to live under His authority, implying that He expects obedience. His preface to His covenant in Exodus 19:5 is explicit: "Now therefore if you will *obey* my voice and *keep* my covenant, you shall be my own possession among all peoples." Israel's election is clearly conditioned on her willingness to live under His authority and walk in obedience to His word. The initial response of Israel to this condition was positive. "All the people answered together and said, 'All the Lord has spoken we will do'" (Ex. 19:8).

The full implication of living under the authority of God begins to be spelled out in the covenant section (Ex. 19–24). After the introduction of the covenant in Exodus 19, God gives the Ten Commandments (Ex. 20) as the basis of His standard of righteous conduct and character. The Ten Commandments or Ten Words are actually principles that relate individuals both to God and to other people. It is as though God were saying, "If you are going to live under my authority, you will have to walk in obedience to these directions for your life." This section is followed by Exodus 21–23 where particularized applications of the ten principles for everyday life are laid out for those under the covenant. To live under God's authority is not to deal only in broad general principles but in applications to life in more specific and significant detail. Submission to God's authority implies that He will rule over all matters both large and small.

It is significant that in this section for the first time the actual words of God are written down (Ex. 24:4). This means that the authority of God over the lives of His covenant people from henceforth is bound up with the written Word of God that has come to us in the holy Scriptures. The basic principle involved is that to live under God's authority is to live under the authority of His written Word. One cannot continue in an intimate covenant relationship with the Lord or with God's people without meeting this condition.

While Israel's initial response to God is to submit to His authority, Moses gives the people an additional opportunity to respond after the principles of obedience and the details of their application are further spelled out. Exodus 24 describes the sealing of the covenant by blood, at which time Moses told the people "all the words of the Lord and all the ordinances." Their response to this larger revelation of what it would mean to live under God's authority was a commitment to walk in obedience to Him. "All the words which the Lord has spoken we will do," they answer (Ex. 24:3). To be certain that there was no misunderstanding about the implications of living under God's authority, Moses took the book of the covenant and read it in the hearing of the people. A third time they responded, "All the Lord has spoken we will do, and we will be obedient" (Ex. 24:7). From that moment on, the written Word of God became the normative authority for God's people, to which Word they looked as the voice of their King.

Living under God's authority is not an end in itself. It is, rather, a means of accomplishing those major objectives God set before His people. Unless men are willing to live under the authority of God and His Word, however, God cannot make them into a kingdom of priests or a holy people. His people find it essential to be guided by God's Word in order to be trained in ministry. Further, God cannot shape the character of His servants or make them holy as He is holy unless they are willing to do what He asks. Obedience to His standard of righteousness is essential for those who would be holy. Thus living under the authority of God and His Word is a necessary means of accomplishing His objectives, of establishing a kingdom of priests serving Him in ministry, and of establishing a holy nation reflecting His character.

THE MEANS TO ACCOMPLISH GOD'S OBJECTIVES: LIVING IN FELLOWSHIP

The second means of accomplishing God's objectives is *living in fellowship with others who seek to follow God.* In Exodus, God speaks to a *nation* of people. This means that His relationship to them and His Word to them is as to individuals in a group. Even in Genesis where the primary focus of the story is God's relationship to six men, it is always to six men and their families. In Exodus it becomes more evident that God wishes to relate to individuals, but He wants to relate to them as a community of people who will follow after Him. The significance of this essential means of following God—fellowship with like-minded people—is often overlooked.

The need for fellowship is rooted in the nature of humanity as created in the image of a triune God (Gen. 1:26–27). God is a social being, three Persons in one Godhead. In the Trinity, God reveals His social nature which is the basis of three things essential for all persons: love, communication, and fellowship. These needs characterize all men and women because they are created in the image of One who displayed these elements as a part of His essential trinitarian nature.

God first reveals mankind's social need in Genesis 2 with the recognition that man is incomplete in himself without woman. The close person-to-person relationship within the family consequently is an expression of the social nature of God and a reflection of His image. But the traditional family is not the only source for meeting this need for intimate personal relationships. The community of faith, or the spiritual family, the extension of the traditional family, is the other most natural expression. People are made for a close fellowship with others who share the same objectives in life and whom they can love and with whom they can communicate and enter into deep relationships. Genesis 2 indicates that God's drawing people together to follow Him is His deliberate design. He intends to meet a basic need He built into people when He created them in His own image.

Living in fellowship is an essential means in God's economy for accomplishing the objectives He has set before His people. Close relationships with a few others of like mind are essential in training for ministry. In the community of faith, believers need one another to hear and understand the Word of God and to learn to communicate it effectively. Training in and growth of important relational skills to bring people into a right relationship with God and help them grow spiritually can occur only in this situation.

Further, believers need the support and aid of an intimate fellowship of like-minded people to develop a holy character. Sharpening, encouraging, building one another up, and holding one another accountable to God's Word enable God's grace to work to transform character.

God directs us to live under His authority and that means obedience to His standard of righteousness. Second, He directs us to live in fellowship with others in a covenant commitment. This requires loving and communicating with others. It is particularly interesting that obedience and love are the two chief responses that a holy God seeks in a people who are to reflect His character (Ex. 20:6; Deut. 7:9).

THE MEANS TO ACCOMPLISH GOD'S OBJECTIVES: LIVING BY FAITH

A third means to God's ends is *faith*. In Exodus God has already laid a basis of evidence for the faith of those whom He invites into a covenant relationship. Both His power and goodness appear in His deliverance of Israel, while He has especially shown His goodness in His gracious care in the desert (Ex. 13–18). So Israel has solid grounds for confidence in God. The covenant offer is built on substantial evidence that this God can be trusted. When the people respond positively to God's initial offer of the covenant, He sends Moses back to them to tell of the coming of His own presence so that "the people may hear when I speak with you and they also believe you forever" (Ex. 19:9). Since Moses speaks God's Word for Him, God's concern is that they believe Moses. Underlying that concern, however, is the desire that they believe God Himself.

Israel's faith is evident in their following God into the wilderness and trusting in His provision for their needs during the previous three months. But this offer of a covenant commitment will involve a deeper level of belief, perhaps more adequately described as a deeper level of trust in God. In a sense this "means" underlies the other two. Their willingness to trust God further leads to a willingness to commit themselves to a deeper level of obedience and to commit themselves to others also seeking to follow the Lord. Trust in God is perhaps the most basic of all responses to Him, but it must then lead to the further responses of obedience and love. A covenant commitment demands deeper trust as the basis of a decision to move into a fuller commitment to God.

Faith as a means of growth is related to God's objectives in two ways. Unless people trust God, they will be unwilling for God to train them for service. Further, unless they deeply trust the nature of God, they will be unwilling for God to work in their lives to reshape their character. Deeper levels of trust in God, then, are linked to all of God's other work in individuals. This is precisely the choice to which He calls

Israel at Sinai—to trust Him in the deeper way. The principle is clear: *when God moves people into greater covenant commitments to Himself and with others, a deeper level of faith in Him is essential.*

THE HEART OF THE COVENANT: THE PERSONAL PRESENCE OF GOD

Finally, there is one more factor closely related to both means and objectives for the people of God, something more difficult to classify: *the personal presence of God among His people.* This is intimately tied to all their relationships to Him. In one sense, His presence is another life objective, i.e., that men should know Him and enjoy His presence. In another sense this relationship is a means of accomplishing God's purposes—creating a kingdom of priests and a holy nation. Only by living in His presence and enjoying an intimate relationship with Him can God's grace work in lives to accomplish His objectives. In the whole presentation of objectives and means, God is concerned that those who enter into covenant with Him do so based upon a living relationship with His personal presence.

In the story of Sinai, this dimension of covenant relationship is graphically illustrated when God comes down on the mountain accompanied by signs and symbols that signal His presence among His people. He says to Moses, "I am coming to you" (Ex. 19:9). The event is vividly told: thick clouds, thunder, lightning, blasts of trumpets, smoke, and quaking mountains. The people respond in fear and awe because a holy God is not to be taken lightly. Yet even before He manifests Himself in His awesome majesty, He has already disclosed Himself in redeeming power, loving care, and in personal, verbal communication with His people.

The unique element in God's coming in Exodus 19 is not sights and sounds, but the remarkable theological fact that He desires to dwell among His people and to cultivate intimate relationships with them. He is the transcendent, supernatural God who, with His power and majesty, is not lightly approached. Yet at the same time He chooses to live among His people and enter into fellowship with them. This is one of the unique features of Israel's God as distinguished from other gods in the ancient Near Eastern world: He is both transcendent and immanent, supernatural and personal, a God who is high and lifted up but who also comes to dwell among His people. Everyone who is a part of the covenant people must understand that He is the sovereign Creator and Governor of the universe, but also the One who desires to enter into close relationships with those who belong to Him.

In summary, it may be said that to be the covenant people of God means to experience, out of the goodness of His nature, redemption by His grace as well as His provisional care. The experience of covenant requires that people set before themselves God's objectives of 1) a growing relationship with Himself, 2) ministry for Him and service to other people, and 3) the development of a godly character. They must choose as their life objectives His desire for them to be a part of a kingdom of priests and a holy people. If these objectives are to be met, His people must also choose God's means of accomplishing those ends. They must submit themselves to life under His authority as expressed in His written Word, walking in obedience to His revealed standard of righteousness for their lives. In addition, they must elect to live in fellowship with others of like mind and heart, living under His authority and seeking to be trained for His service and shaped in His likeness. They cannot choose any of these unless they are willing to trust God at a deeper level than that required by redeeming grace. They must believe that He is trustworthy. Then by an act of the will they must make a deeper commitment that will involve obedience and love as well as an earnest seeking to fulfill God's purposes for their lives. Finally, to be the covenant people of God means to recognize His sovereign majesty and at the same time to establish a personal, vital relationship with Him: God's people must both know Him and seek to live in His presence.

2

Ծisciples of Jesus

THE OLD COVENANT: CONTEXT FOR THE
NEW COVENANT

Similarities between the establishment of the New Covenant and the Old are remarkable. What God did when He commenced the making of "a people of His own possession" at Sinai, He continues to do with the giving of the New Covenant through the ministry of Jesus. The Gospel of Matthew is particularly helpful in showing the continuity of God's purposes in this regard. Matthew wrote for a Jewish audience. His design was to convince them that the Jesus he describes was the Messiah for whom they had looked so many centuries. He lays the foundation of his case at the outset of his Gospel with Jesus' genealogy. Beginning with Abraham, he traces the line of descent all the way to Jesus. For any knowledgeable Jew it would have been an easily understood reminder of the history of God's plans and purposes throughout Israel's existence.

Further, Matthew records the greatest number of citations from the Old Testament to be found in any of the Gospels. The author carefully calls attention to key events in the life, teaching, and ministry of Jesus. Matthew regards these events as part of the fulfillment of God's purpose and plan throughout the history of His people. Consequently, when Matthew introduces the public ministry of Jesus, he does so by quoting one of the great messianic passages of the Old Testament (Isa. 9:1–2; Matt. 4:14–16). Clearly, he is making his case that Jesus is the Messiah.

It is not surprising, then, that in the opening description of Jesus' ministry Matthew meticulously points out symbolic parallels between the initial giving of the New Covenant and that of the Old. As the Old Covenant was given to the twelve tribes of Israel, Jesus draws about Him twelve disciples to represent the new Israel of God. Whereas the people of God under the Old Covenant were led by a pair of brothers, Jesus, in His leadership training under the New Covenant, chooses two sets of brothers. Just as Moses ascended a mountain to receive the Old Covenant, Jesus climbs a mountain, sets His disciples down, and teaches them the heart of the New Covenant (Matt. 5:1ff.). In the Old Testament, those who were in a covenant relationship with the Lord were known as the people of God. In the New Testament they are known as the disciples of Jesus. The mention of these parallels is Matthew's way of reinforcing the continuity between God's purposes under the Old Covenant and under the New. In light of this, it is not surprising that in describing Jesus' opening ministry Matthew also emphasizes the similarity between God's objectives and means under the new age with His design under the old dispensation.

BASIS OF DISCIPLESHIP:
REDEMPTION BY GRACE

Matthew begins to describe the principles of discipleship in chapter 4, making clear that the first requirement is an experience of personal redemption by the grace of God. At the opening of His public ministry, Jesus calls sinners to saving grace when He cries, "Repent, for the kingdom of heaven is at hand" (Matt. 4:17). Matthew makes his case that accepting God's rule in their lives is essential for would-be disciples.

Mark makes the picture even clearer in his selection of

material from Jesus' early preaching: "The time is fulfilled, the kingdom of God is at hand; repent and believe the gospel" (Mark 1:15). A positive response to the announcement of the gospel and a commitment to God's kingly rule are essential for those who want to come into a right relationship with God and begin to follow after Him. Mark clearly spells out the conditions of this experience of God's saving grace: repentance and faith. Individuals must turn away from their sins and trust God to work in their lives. A more nearly complete depiction of the gospel message as well as the conditions of repentance and belief are delineated in the Gospels and Epistles. Yet this initial presentation recorded by Mark opens Jesus' ministry and indicates the necessity of this step—starting with a right relationship—if hearers are to become disciples of the Lord. Unless one repents of his sins and believes the gospel, no way remains for him to begin the journey toward discipleship.

THE DISTINCTION BETWEEN A BELIEVER AND A DISCIPLE

In the same context in which he introduced conditions for entering the kingdom of God, Matthew shows that repentance and belief in the gospel do not automatically make one a disciple of Jesus. Many believed in the Lord who were not His disciples either in the primary or secondary sense of the word. This has led to confusion throughout the history of the church. Some have assumed that repentance and belief automatically made them disciples of Jesus. But in the biblical record, Jesus calls first for repentance and faith; then, second, as a separate event He calls believers to follow Him as disciples (Matt. 4:17–22; Mark 1:14–20). This twofold pattern parallels the Old Testament model in which God first delivered Israel from Egypt and then, three months later, offered them a covenant relationship with Himself at Sinai. It is one thing to trust God initially and begin to follow Him, but it is quite another to commit oneself to a covenant relationship with God and become a disciplined follower.

Those choosing to be part of the covenant people of God and follow as disciples of Jesus must discover—and emulate—the biblical principles of discipleship. Accordingly, the focus of this study is not primarily on conversion or the process of evangelism that brings people to repentance and faith in the Lord. Rather, the emphasis is on that next stage of commitment to which Jesus desires to draw believers in order to make them disciplined followers or disciples. With this in mind, I will employ the word discipleship to refer to that pattern of Jesus' actions that occurs with the men He drew to Himself after they had believed on Him.

OBJECTIVES OF DISCIPLESHIP: SERVICE FOR GOD

As Jesus begins to call and instruct disciples, the parallel with God's objectives under the Old Covenant becomes immediately apparent. Jesus' command, "Follow me, and I will make you fishers of men" (Matt. 4:19), shows that one of His objectives is to train His followers for ministry. "I will make you fishers of men" indicates Jesus' plan to enable His disciples spiritually to touch the lives of other people. Spoken in language they easily understand, His meaning is clear. He is binding a group of men to Himself in order to fit them for service to others on His behalf. While the reference to disciples as fishers of men might suggest evangelism and outreach, the context of the Gospel reveals Jesus' plans for a broader scope of training. Thus when He begins to concentrate on teaching, Jesus instructs them about their role as salt and light in the world (Matt. 5:13–16). Later He trains them for public ministry—teaching, preaching, and healing (Matt. 9:35). Jesus' training culminates in His charge to the Twelve to be disciple-makers (Matt. 28:19–20).

From the outset, the Lord indicates that His disciples will be expected to serve as He serves. The discipleship process is part of their training, and they cannot be disciples without involvement in active ministry. Significantly the Lord chose working men to be His disciples. He did not pick the idle, the lazy, nor those who were unwilling to live purposefully. He begins with their willingness to work and then transforms that willingness into desire to serve Him by touching the world for God.

One lesson that those who become disciples must learn is that serving Him takes precedence over every other work in their lives. Called to leave their boats and nets, the Twelve choose to leave their businesses and their livelihoods. As disciples of Jesus they must learn to trust Him to provide not only their own needs, but those of their families while they spend their time and energy in ministry with and for Him. The principle is the same for all who desire to be disciples. While Jesus does not require all to leave their secular occupations to become disciples, the real work to which Jesus calls them will be to a spiritual ministry. All other employment must be subsumed under that larger purpose. To become a disciple requires one 1) to assent to let Jesus choose a life work, and 2) to be responsible for investing one's time and energy under His direction. Jesus will not, indeed, cannot make believers into disciples when they are unwilling to follow Him in this way.

OBJECTIVES OF DISCIPLESHIP: HOLINESS OF CHARACTER

The second of God's major objectives also appears under the New Covenant and is bound up with Jesus' command to follow Him (Matt. 4:19). When Jesus calls, His desire is to make His followers like Himself. He wants to shape their character so that they will reflect His character in the world. It is as though He were saying, "Come, let me make you like me." And this is precisely what He begins to do. From this point He concentrates on their attitudes, motivations, personal relationships, and conduct. For instance, He delineates a number of these essential principles in the Beatitudes (Matt. 5:3–12). After setting out these general principles, Jesus focuses on the two traits most closely related to moral holiness when He lays before them a standard of righteousness (Matt. 5:20–42) and a challenge to love (Matt. 5:43–48). Although Jesus does not use the word *holiness* in Matthew 4 or 5, it is clear to those familiar with the content of the Old Covenant that God desires righteous living and loving hearts as the chief expressions of that holy character the Lord wants (Ex. 20:6; Deut. 7:9; Lev. 19:2, 15–18).

There is no question but that the Holy One of Israel has most perfectly revealed His character in the person of His Son. John expresses this when he writes, "No one has ever seen God; the only Son, who is in the bosom of the Father, He has made Him known" (John 1:18). Again, Paul notes that Jesus, the "image of the invisible God" (Col. 1:15), is the full revelation of God's holy character. This underlies the angel's word to Mary that when the Holy Spirit comes upon her, "the child to be born will be called holy, the Son of God" (Luke 1:35). It is apparent that the disciples have learned that Jesus is the full reflection of God's holy nature when they confess, "We have believed, and have come to know, that you are the Holy One of God" (John 6:69).

This is why those who are particularly concerned about holiness of heart and life have often described godly character as Christlikeness. Jesus gives us a picture of holiness with a human face. He fully reveals God's character as well as the character that God plans for His people. Originally created in the image of God, we now see in Jesus what that image is meant to be. From the opening of His ministry, Jesus binds men to himself to shape their character. He wants them to be like the Father and like Himself; further, He reveals His desire for them to be like the Holy Spirit. He teaches from the beginning that the chief expressions of this holy character will be in their righteousness and love.

MEANS TO ACCOMPLISH GOD'S OBJECTIVES: LIVING UNDER AUTHORITY

If, under the New Covenant, life objectives are the same as under the Old, a parallel pattern emerges regarding the means to achieve those intentions. Jesus makes clear that *living under the authority of God and His Word* is still essential. He begins by inviting men to enter into the kingdom or, stated in other words, to come under the kingship of God (Matt. 4:17). He emphasizes God's kingly rule and the implications of life under that kingship (Matt. 4:23; 5:19–20). God, who desired to be King over people's lives under the Old Covenant, still desires the same under the New. The fresh dimension of this concept, however, is that the kingship of God is immediately present in the person of Jesus. Those who desire to live under God's kingly rule now must live under the rule of Jesus. The implications of this for disciples are first revealed with Jesus' call to them when He said, "Follow me" (Matt. 4:19), a command that they must either obey or reject. On the outcome of this decision rests the whole process of discipleship. For the disciples to place themselves under the authority of Jesus means to place themselves under the authority of God and of the living Word (John 1:1, 14, 18).

In addition to life under His authority, Jesus also teaches His disciples that they are to continue under the authority of the written Word of God as it then existed: "Think not that I have come to abolish the law or the prophets; I have not come to abolish them but to fulfill them" (Matt. 5:17). Jesus could neither train His disciples for ministry nor shape their character into His own likeness, if they were unwilling to submit to this means of His working in their lives.

This principle continues to be true for all who would be disciples. The Word of God must become the practical authority for all Christian disciples. In one sense, the triune God is really the final authority for the people of God. Yet in practice He has left this to His disciples in His normative Word, the holy Scriptures. Thus for the everyday living out of discipleship, those seeking to be disciplined followers of Jesus must live in the Word of God to be under His authority at all times.

MEANS TO ACCOMPLISH GOD'S OBJECTIVES: LIVING IN RELATIONSHIP

The second means of accomplishing God's objectives in the disciples is that of *living in close fellowship with other disciples*. Jesus does not call and train disciples in isolation from one another. He does not have one disciple in Nazareth, another in Cana, a third in Capernaum, a fourth in Tiberias, and several down in Jerusalem. Rather, He calls a group to follow Him, and He trains them together.

Jesus builds carefully on the inner need of all men for intimate fellowship with a few others of similar life purpose and commitment. It is probably deliberate that He draws to Himself two sets of brothers: Peter and Andrew, James and John. The four already had developed a close relationship; Luke adds that they were partners in a fishing business. This means that Jesus began with a core of men who were already socially close. Then He proceeded to transform these already established relationships into a profound spiritual fellowship. At the same time, He satisfied a deep personal need in their lives.

Further, it seems likely that Jesus used the traditional family as a model for His discipleship group. The basic dynamics of family include intimate personal relationships, communication, love, commitment, support, encouragement, and loyalty to one another. All of these are a part of Jesus' design for the spiritual family of disciples.

This strategy for accomplishing God's ends provides several insights. One is that while every member of the fellowship is cultivating a relationship with Jesus, each is simultaneously cultivating a relationship with every other member of the band. Disciples need to relate to members as well as to the leader and model of the group.

Another insight is that the group is small because of the need to relate closely to a few other people. Intimacy demands a significant commitment of spiritual and emotional energy as well as time. No one has enough of either time or energy to get to know a large group of people well. In fact, it was possible for a group of twelve to get to know each other intimately only because they lived together constantly.

Contemporary discipleship groups will want to number fewer than twelve in order to get the time necessary to develop close personal relationships. From Jesus' perspective it is only when His followers live in this close fellowship with a few others of like mind that He is able to fulfill God's objectives for their lives. We are best trained for ministry and service for God in a fellowship of persons who are being trained in the same way. In a similar fashion, character is shaped like the character of Jesus only when we are with those who also seek with all their hearts to follow Him. Thus the context of a spiritual family is essential both for effective service for God and for reflecting His likeness in the world.

MEANS TO ACCOMPLISH GOD'S OBJECTIVES: LIVING BY FAITH

A third means of God's working in the lives of the disciples is presupposed in the early chapters of the gospel story. It is faith. Coupled with repentance, faith is required for entrance into the kingdom of God (Mark 1:15). But a second and deeper level of faith underlies a response to Jesus' command to follow Him. Those who decide to follow Jesus as the disciples did choose to place their lives under His authority and live in a relationship with Him like that of first-century disciples with their rabbi. In the New Testament that involved confidence that Jesus was trustworthy and that He could be trusted to shape and train them for service. Thus in many places where the term *faith* is not used, trust in the Lord is implied. Unless men are willing to trust Him, and consequently become dependent upon Him, He cannot prepare them for their life work nor make them what they ought to be.

THE HEART OF DISCIPLESHIP: LIVING IN THE PERSONAL PRESENCE OF JESUS

Finally, under the New Covenant lies a key element that is at the same time both an objective and a means: living in the presence of God in the person of Jesus and developing an in-depth relationship with Him. When Jesus says to the disciples, "Follow me," He is binding them to an intimate relationship with Himself. They are to follow *Him*. To be a disciple of Jesus is not primarily to go through a program of training but to learn to know a Person.

One of God's objectives for the Twelve was that they would learn to live constantly in His presence, and to grasp the principle well enough so that they would continue to live in His presence and cultivate that relationship even after Jesus' Ascension.

Enjoying life in the presence of Jesus is, in a sense, a life objective in itself. Yet in another way, it is also God's means of preparing them for ministry and of shaping their character. Precisely because of their relationship with Him, Jesus can train them to serve God, communicate His Word, and bring others into a saving relationship with the Father. Further, it is Jesus who develops godly character in them. Character is developed over time. So this time is not just spent; it is invested because He is shaping and molding them into His own likeness. Without an intimate personal relationship with Jesus, it is impossible for God to make us like Himself.

SUMMARY OF THE OBJECTIVES AND MEANS OF DISCIPLESHIP

The principles of discipleship for the followers of Jesus, then, are basically the same as those for the Old Testament covenant people of God. Salvation by grace is the beginning and may be described as entering the kingdom of heaven or starting to follow Jesus. The conditions are repentance and faith.

But those who want to follow on as Jesus' disciples will go further and commit themselves to God's basic life objectives. They must be willing to be trained for a life of service. They will be trained to be fishers of men, and salt and light in the world—preachers, teachers, servants, disciple-makers. They will begin to reflect the character of God as revealed in Jesus. Characteristics of His life will become theirs, especially as His holy nature is revealed in righteousness and love.

Disciples of Jesus will choose to live under the authority of God as revealed in the living Word of Jesus and the written Word of God of both Old and New Testaments. They will walk in obedience to Jesus in all that He says and in all that the Father has written down for them in the holy Scriptures. They will also choose to live in an intimate fellowship with others who also want to be disciples. They will cultivate those relationships as well as their relationship to the Lord, and be bonded together in a fellowship of love. They will learn that their commitment to discipleship involves a deeper level of trust in the Lord than that which brought them to saving grace. They will go from faith to faith, trusting Jesus in ever greater measure. Finally, they will learn to live continuously in His presence, having as a major life task the cultivation of their relationship with Him. While enjoying His presence, they will allow Him to use that presence for His own purposes in their lives.

3

qualifications for discipleship

THE PERSON AND WORK OF JESUS

The first chapter of John's gospel is designed as a theological introduction to the person and work of Jesus. In the prologue (1:1–18) he describes Jesus as co-creator with God (1:1–3) and as the Word from God to men (1:1, 4–5, 9, 14, 18). John portrays Jesus as the source of life and light (1:4–5) as well as the One who gives power to individuals, enabling them to become members of the family of God (1:12–13). Further, Jesus is shown to be the Word become flesh, dwelling among men and revealing God's glory (1:14).

In the latter part of chapter 1 the writer relates incidents from the life of John the Baptist as another means to introduce Jesus. The Baptist's ministry is preparatory to the coming of Jesus, but his preaching also serves to help his listeners understand what God is going to do through Jesus. In this vein, the Gospel enumerates three major elements of Jesus' work: 1) His death, 2) His sending of the Holy Spirit, 3) His disciplemaking. These are present not only in the work that Jesus did in His own day, they are part of the work He wants to do for every Christian in each generation.

THE WORK OF JESUS: DEATH ON THE CROSS

John identifies the first element of Jesus' work in his statement to his disciples that Jesus is "the Lamb of God, who takes away the sin of the world" (1:29, 36). The reference to Jesus as a lamb looks forward to His sacrificial death on the cross. From the very beginning John is preparing readers for the story's conclusion. His point is that Jesus has come into the world, not just as a good example, but to die and to give His life as a ransom for many. This Gospel's thrust is that through the Atonement Jesus makes available an experience of saving grace for everyone.

The historical event of Christ's death has a contemporary relevance because God wants everyone to experience His redeeming grace, to know the forgiveness of sins, and to come into new life in Him. Simply put, this is the beginning of discipleship. No one can be Christ's disciple without having Christ come into his or her life to forgive sins, cleanse the heart from guilt, and be drawn into a new relationship with the Father. Jesus made all this possible on the basis of His death on the cross. The first step in the process is an experience of His saving grace.

THE WORK OF JESUS: SENDING THE HOLY SPIRIT

However, John the Baptist speaks not only about the Cross. He describes how the Father revealed to him that Jesus would send the Holy Spirit. "He on whom you see the Spirit descend and remain, this is He who baptizes with the Holy Spirit" (John 1:33). This statement is repeated in all four Gospels and Acts. Five times it is stated in Scripture that Jesus will baptize with the Spirit, i.e., send the Spirit to dwell in His fullness within the disciples. This particular work of Jesus, of course, was completed on the day of Pentecost when He poured out the Spirit upon those disciples who waited in the Upper Room.

The foretelling of this event in the context of the

disciples' call suggests that Jesus wants to see this experience repeated in the life of every disciple in every age. The implications will be discussed at length in following chapters; it is sufficient now only to mention John's suggestion that the experience will go beyond, and will certainly follow, the experience of saving grace. It will both signify and make available a deeper, more nearly complete relationship with God.

THE WORK OF JESUS: MAKING DISCIPLES

In much of the church two aspects of the work of Jesus have been crucial points for preaching and teaching. First, men and women have been called to saving grace, brought to an experience of justification and the new birth. Second, a call to the deeper commitment of the baptism of the Holy Spirit has often followed in order that Christians might know the fullness of God's Spirit through surrender to Christ and His lordship over them. These two points of commitment have been emphasized. But John the Baptist introduces a third element in Jesus' ministry which, though closely related, has not received the same attention in our day. Yet John the Evangelist indicates that this emphasis of Jesus' ministry is just as significant in accomplishing what Jesus wants in the lives of His followers.

The third aspect has to do with following Jesus. The disciples who are introduced in John 1 began to follow Jesus when Andrew, and probably John, came to see what He was like (John 1:37–39). When Jesus spoke to Philip, He said, "Follow me" (John 1:43). Then they left with Him for Galilee to begin that process of spiritual training which may properly be called discipleship. Thus, *discipling* was the third major work that Jesus began. While the elements of saving grace and the baptism of the Holy Spirit are point-in-time experiences, this part of Jesus' plan is a matter of growth and training. It took our Lord three years of life-to-life investment to accomplish His desire: to pour His life into the lives of twelve men. Discipleship is not a static event or condition but a process that occurs because His life is being transferred to other lives over a period of days, months, and years. Jesus invested His life in these men. When He finished, He said in effect, "Go and do the same thing in another's life."

CHARACTERISTICS OF POTENTIAL DISCIPLES

One of the great values of the first chapter of John's gospel is its indication of the kind of people Jesus sought to disciple. The qualities He seems to have looked for are worth study. New Testament discipleship, we discover, can take place among only a few people. When Jesus came, though hundreds listened to Him, only several dozen followed after Him to the end of His life. Out of that group He picked twelve to be His disciples. Why did He select this particular band of men over all the others? What was it about them that made Him choose them for training? What qualifications did they possess that we should look for in believers now if the Lord is going to make disciples today as well? The first chapter of John gives us certain clues.

Hunger for God

First, these men shared a hunger for God. The picture of John the Baptist preaching in the wilderness and of people going out to see him is a reminder that he spearheaded the first spiritual revival in Israel in four centuries. As he preached repentance and forgiveness, people flocked to hear him. Apparently Andrew and probably John, the writer of this Gospel, were two of those who responded to the Baptist's preaching. Not only did they respond, coming to forgiveness and a commitment to God, they also attached themselves to John as disciples. They became disciplined followers of the last of the Old Testament prophets. They were not on the fringes of the crowd around the Baptist. This could not have been accidental. These men were already committed because they had a heart hunger for God. Something about them wanted what God had for them. In John the Baptist they saw God working, and they desired to be a part of it. So they sought him out and spent time with him. Then when John said, "God is going to do something unusual through this person, this Jesus," they responded again.

God still looks for men and women who hunger to be where God is working, hungry for Him to do something for them. They are willing to place themselves in situations and relationships so that God can work within and through them. Some in the church today believe that a desire for God is simply something that certain people have and others do not. For them such hunger is an arbitrary gift from God that He dispenses to a few and withholds from others. This certainly does not fit the biblical picture of God's work with His people. The Bible does not describe God as arbitrarily choosing to give some a deep appetite for spiritual things and withholding it from others. Rather, God gives to all persons grace to choose for Him to continue His shaping and reshaping work in their lives.

Because of God's grace at work in every life, all people have the privilege of choosing to let more grace work in their hearts and in relationships with Him. People are hungry for God because they choose to hunger after Him. More explicitly, they choose a series of actions or attitudes that make it possible for God to work more significantly in their lives. If one has a spiritual hunger, it is because he or she chooses it.

What is the evidence that one is choosing to hunger after God in this way? One indicator is that such a person wants to be in places where God is working. Such individuals long to be where God's people are gathered. They desire to read that which will feed their souls. They enjoy the kind of music that will lift their spirits. They are serious about the use of their energy and their leisure time. Often they cannot fully explain it, but they sense a drive to get where God is working, where God's people are. They decide that it is a priority matter because they want to be numbered among the disciples of Jesus. If one qualification for discipleship stands out, this would be it: God is looking for men and women who hunger after Him and have a heart for Him. Jesus says to all such persons, "Blessed are those who hunger and thirst for righteousness" (Matt. 5:6).

Availability

The second characteristic of the men Jesus chose is their willingness to be available. They took time from their fishing business to seek after God. They made time to be with John so that when he points them to Jesus they are eager to seek Jesus and spend time with Him. "They came and saw where He was staying, and they stayed *with* Him that day for it was about the tenth hour" (John 1:39, emphasis mine). They were with Jesus the rest of the day. They were available to be with Him; available to enjoy His presence.

It is impossible to be a disciple of Jesus without making time available for the process. Many would like to be counted among his close followers; they would like to have an intimate relationship with Jesus, but are unwilling to make spending time with him a priority in their overcrowded schedules. In such a case, discipleship is impossible. The New Testament shows that availability is essential to discipleship. This means that some things must be a priority in personal schedules, viz., a relationship with God and with the people whom God is using in their lives.

The chief reason a disciple needs to be available is to cultivate his relationship with Jesus. The development of this relationship cannot continue without extended time spent in His presence. The Twelve were available. They became available at the outset of Jesus' ministry (John 1), and they remained available for the next three years. It took time for Jesus to make these men into His disciples; it takes time for Him to do similar things in our lives today. As a result, it is a distinct advantage to be a member for several years of a discipleship group. Only then can God do certain key things in each member's life, and only then can they adequately learn the process of investing their own lives in other people. God teaches disciples many things from the people that He has put around them, and He teaches many of those things the second year (or the third or fourth) that could not be learned the first.

Not only did those whom Jesus drew about Him have time with Him; they had time with each other. This is the other side of discipleship. Christians must not only cultivate their relationship with the Lord, they must cultivate their relationships with other disciples in order to let the others have a proper influence on them. There may be some lessons one has mastered that others have yet to learn, even the disciplemaker. The question is whether disciples are willing to spend enough time with others so they may learn. Making time available is the key.

Faithfulness

The third qualification for becoming a disciple has to do with faithfulness. The men Jesus called demonstrated faithfulness from the first. They had lived with John the Baptist and were committed to him, but when John pointed them to Jesus, they responded. When they learned something new about Jesus, they faithfully passed it on. Andrew went after Peter to bring him to Jesus; it may be assumed that John sought out his brother James. They immediately shared the things that God showed them. In the same manner, Philip, immediately after Jesus called him, looked for Nathanael (John 1:43–45). While only their initial faithfulness can be seen in this context, the Gospels reveal a picture of continuing learning and faithfulness in their following the Master.

Faithfulness to Jesus is not automatic. It is possible to begin with Him and then to go back on one's commitment. People can be disciples of Jesus, a part of a fellowship, committed followers and yet, at some point, like Judas, decide to go some way other than God's. They can take themselves out of the discipleship process and even out of the saving relationship with Jesus. Not everyone who breaks the discipling relationship severs the total connection with Jesus as Judas did. But it is possible. Heaven is not guaranteed simply by membership in a disciples' band. Continuing faith and faithfulness are crucial here.

Teachability

The last thing this passage reveals about the disciples is that they were teachable. They were characterized by an openness of spirit. John announced, "Behold, the Lamb of God," and they responded to his direction immediately. They went to Jesus and addressed Him as rabbi or teacher. Jesus said, "What are you looking for?" They replied, "We want to talk. We want to see where you are staying." They spent the rest of the day with Him and left toward evening feeling that He may well have been the Messiah for whom they particularly but also all Israel had been looking. Immediately they began to tell others what they had learned. This is the kind of openness of spirit that distinguishes those for whom the Lord is looking.

Right after the story about the teachability of Andrew and John comes the introduction of Philip. He responds to Jesus' call, going immediately to find his friend Nathanael. Nathanael is skeptical. "Can any good thing come out of Nazareth?" But his questions are direct and open, and Jesus notes that he is an Israelite "in whom there is no guile," or as we might say, "in whom is no underhandedness." He is straightforward, but he is teachable. When he comes to Jesus and discovers that this Nazarene knows something about him that he thought was hidden and that He can see into his heart and life, Nathanael's skepticism vanishes. He is willing to be convinced and so he learns quickly.

An important difference exists between teachability and gullibility. Jesus is not looking for people to swallow any idea that comes along. Hebrews is clear that one of the marks of spiritual maturity is ability to discern good from evil, right from wrong, and truth from error (5:13–14). Jesus develops in disciples just such an ability, but He can do it only if they are teachable.

Members of a discipleship group are not always going to

agree, even in a close fellowship. While they learn to agree more and more frequently as they live and grow together, they will never agree on everything. Yet each disciple wants to be able to say, "What is the Lord saying to me? How is He using this fellowship and this teaching from the Word to talk to me?" It may be that the leader of a fellowship is a peer, and the Enemy may tempt the disciples to say, "This guy is just like me"; or "She is just another wife like me. Who is she to tell me?" Disciples with this attitude are sure to miss something significant that Jesus has for them to learn.

Different people, of course, have different temperaments. People learn and respond differently. But teachability is not related so much to temperament as it is to a choice of the will. We can choose to be open or closed to what God has to say. It is as though the Lord says, "I am looking for those who are open to me and willing for me to use leaders of discipleship groups and brothers or sisters in those fellowships to say something to them."

In discipleship fellowships some find it easier than others to tell about themselves, what they feel, and what they have learned. Some leaders also find it easier to speak from the heart, and certain disciples will find it easier to learn from them. But not everyone operates in the same way, and even some leaders need to be drawn out. Both a teachable spirit and a bit of aggressiveness about wanting to learn are essential. The chief way to practice "active learning" is to ask questions. For example, someone may need to say, "What do you think about this? Why did Jesus say that? Where is this principle found in Scripture? How do I go about applying this to my life? What is happening with you and your family?" It is like having a well; one needs to let down the bucket and draw some things out—both from wells and from people. It is true that many important ideas, thoughts, burdens may be on the surface; but more important issues may be below the surface. It may take some work to draw them out. That demands both work and time. It does not happen overnight.

But the one who is willing to draw others out, the one eager to listen, is usually the one with the teachable spirit.

SUMMARY OF QUALIFICATIONS

When Jesus looks for potential disciples, He is looking for those who have a heart for God, are available to be with Him, willing to seek Him, faithful in their commitments, and teachable. Those who come with this kind of spirit and attitude are candidates to be Jesus' disciples. He can make them into disciplined followers just as He did the Twelve. He can shape their characters to be like Himself, and He can prepare them for His service. Not many are among that company. The Gospels suggest a ratio of about a dozen disciples to the several hundred who heard Him and followed at some distance. But he still looks for those who want God to do in them everything He did for Jesus' first discipleship band.

4

means to discipleship

As we have seen, the biblical picture of God's objectives for Jesus' disciples is Christlikeness of character, fruitfulness in service, and an intimate relationship with the Lord. His chief means to accomplish these ends are the experiences of saving grace, sanctifying grace, and growth in grace. In other words, to reach God's ends disciples must be born again, filled with the Holy Spirit, and experience the steps of discipleship. The discipleship process (as explained in this chapter) may be divided into three essential principles: life-to-life transference, spiritual disciplines, and accountability.

THE PRINCIPLE OF LIFE TRANSFERENCE

Life transference occurs when a person shares wisdom, knowledge, experience, and maturity with another. Although learning occurs in structured situations, learning also takes place in informal situations during the normal everyday living of life. Some things are easier caught than taught. This principle, "life transference," where one life is shared with another, is based on the concept of modeling. Most people learn more effectively when they both hear a concept and see it demonstrated (modeled) in a real-life situation. For example, when someone models godliness of character and effective patterns for service, an observer can more easily understand these truths and translate them into his or her own life.

The principle of life transference is modeled for Christians in Jesus' relationship to the Twelve. The Gospels show that when He called them to follow Him, He created an atmosphere in which He could pour His life into theirs. Jesus taught and lived out truth before them. He told His disciples how to minister to others, and gave them concrete examples of how to do it.

By attaching themselves to Jesus, the Twelve entered into an intimate relationship with Him that made possible that transference of His life to theirs. From the beginning of His public ministry, He included a major amount of private, concentrated ministry to those around Him. The Twelve in particular had opportunity to observe His character at close range, and they were able to observe how He ministered to others in a variety of real-life situations.

Time Together

The disciples are with Him full time. When He travels, they go with him; when He preaches and teaches, they sit in the audience; when He heals, they learn how to do it. As Jesus deals with great crowds, they observe how he ministers; when Jesus faces opposition, they learn how to confront and overcome.

Life-to-life transference requires that Jesus spend an enormous amount of time with the men. As is true of any disciplemaker, the more they are all together, the more opportunity He has to model ministry before them. Consequently, one of the crucial qualifications for discipleship is availablity for extended periods with the disciplemaker.

Some of the time spent together should be in formal instruction, but much of it will be in informal situations. For example, time should be invested in ministry so that disciples can learn ministry skills. But then, again, during more informal life situations, disciples learn a good deal about the character of a disciplemaker and draw from the disciplemaker's experience with the Lord. Participants in the process, then, must look both for structured settings to learn from their leader and also for informal time so that from personal conversation and observation they may evaluate the life and work of a disciplemaker.

Some of Jesus' most effective teaching opportunities with the disciples were probably those spent on the road. These would have provided Him occasion to converse freely with the disciples one-on-one where He could discover the needs and problems of those related to Him. It would also include conversations with them in groups of two and three. Further, the hours would provide opportunity for informal direction, questions and answers, and dialogue about spiritual truth. Also the men would find unique opportunities for service. On one occasion as Jesus moved from Galilee down to Jerusalem, a "rich young ruler" approached Him (Matt. 19:16–30). When Jesus set His standard before this young man and he turned away, His disciples were aghast. It is important to note that Jesus spent more time explaining this peculiar response of His to the disciples and enlarging upon the principles involved than He spent with the young man himself.

A second special occasion for informal life-to-life learning takes place in Jesus' ministry during meals. This is a natural setting for conversation and fellowship. Indeed, Jesus' use of mealtimes for teaching has a significant Old Testament precedent. The Hebrew family reserved certain of those occasions for fathers to instruct their children. Meals naturally lend themselves to conversation, especially when several are present, e.g., John 13–16.

Those employing the biblical principle of life-to-life sharing find that informal occasions when people travel or eat together offer natural opportunities for life-changing learning to take place. Because the process is time consuming, such occasions are also a valuable way to multiply time. They provide important opportunities which might not be easily scheduled in the busy hours of a regular day.

Expended Energy

In addition to the time commitment, another costly aspect of life transference is the energy required. Such a process involves spiritual energy that necessitates a spiritual sharpness on the part of the leader. To impart spiritual truth means that disciplemakers themselves must be very intimate in their relationship with God. The process also calls for expenditure of tremendous emotional energy. Disciplemakers must listen carefully if they would understand and try intelligently to meet basic needs of the discipled. Such activity involves the draining process of expending one's psychic energy which is at the heart of life-to-life sharing. Leaders must also be prepared to use up physical energy as demands are made upon them. See John 4 for an example of Jesus investing in His disciples when He was physically and spiritually exhausted.

The tremendous amount of spiritual, psychological, and physical energy necessary for life-to-life transference to take place explains why discipleship can be done only with a few people at a time. No one, including Jesus, has unlimited energy. Because He had taken on the limitations of human flesh when He became the Son of Man, it meant that even though He was God, He had chosen the restrictions of human energy levels. The result was that even Jesus could not disciple more than a dozen men in any intimate way. It is probably significant that out of the twelve He had a still more concentrated investment in three. Even He could not give to the entire group the same investment of life and energy that He did to the three.

The implication is that no disciplemaker can invest in more than a small number of people and still actually do New Testament discipleship. In fact, as I suggested above, for most disciplemakers in our day twelve are too many. Jesus could manage twelve because He had them with Him full time for three years. Most disciplemakers and disciples today do not have that amount of time together. Consequently, today's groups must be smaller, and the process will take longer than it did for Jesus.

Disciples Sharing With Disciples

The last aspect of life-to-life transference as we see it in Scripture shows us that this process not only takes place between Jesus and each member of the discipleship band, it also occurs from one disciple to another. While Jesus walks ahead and takes time with one disciple or perhaps a small group, the other disciples converse among themselves and learn from one another. From the glimpses the Gospels give of their conversations, it is easy to imagine that a great deal of other interaction occurs. The value is in their learning from one another and building on one another's insight, experience, and understanding.

The principle of life-to-life transference in a group is simply an extension of the principle of group learning. People help one another learn because they are social beings. We build on the lives of others as we learn from their experiences. This is part of the New Testament principle of building up one another in the Lord (2 Cor. 10:8; 1 Thess. 5:11).

The point is that everyone must develop relationships with others in the group and not only with the disciplemaker. Multiple relationships are involved, although this results in a drain upon everyone's time and energy. This is yet another reason why discipleship groups cannot be too large; no one has enough time or energy to know a great number of people well, especially at the depth portrayed in the New Testament discipleship process. Still, every member of the family of God has some important things to share from his own life. Those joined together by the Spirit of God need to learn from one another so that the body of Christ might be built up and edified by grace.

The Necessity of Life Transference

Perhaps a warning is in order for those involved in contemporary discipleship experiences. The term "discipleship" has become so popular that it is sometimes carelessly used to describe many different approaches to spiritual formation. A number of current so-called discipleship programs do not include life-to-life sharing. Some involve classes, structured teaching, manuals, and completion of courses. While these have their proper place, the heart of the New Testament practice of discipleship includes a life-to-life sharing process in a variety of life situations over a long period of time. Unless this is included, real biblical discipleship does not happen. Worthwhile things may be learned, helpful concepts may be grasped, people may grow. But unless life is shared with life, discipleship as Jesus did it is not taking place.

THE PRINCIPLE OF
SPIRITUAL DISCIPLINES

In every dimension of life a price has to be paid for anything done well. This is true in developing a relationship with God. Disciples must pay the price of knowing Him well by commitment to certain spiritual disciplines, those regular habit patterns that result in an intimate relationship with God. Then out of that intimate relationship God shapes character. As in any relationship, regularity is necessary for growth, and disciples must devote time and energy if they would know God well and if He is to continue His work of grace in their lives. At the outset of Jesus' ministry with His disciples spiritual disciplines begin to appear as He sets out to build certain life habits into the men. Since He does not list them, it becomes part of our theological task to draw them out from the data.

The Discipline of Time With the Word of God

The first of these principles has already been discussed in a preliminary way, namely, living under the authority of God and His Word. In His earliest teaching, Jesus declares that those who follow Him must submit to the authority of God's revelation in the Old Testament. "'Think not that I have come to abolish the law and the prophets; I have come not to abolish them but to fulfill them; for truly, I say to you, till heaven and earth pass away, not an iota, not a dot, will pass from the law until all is accomplished'" (Matt. 5:17–18). The Twelve are not to imagine that following Jesus somehow gets them around the tough demands of the moral law of God. After making His general statement, Jesus continues to illustrate the full extent of the moral law's application to His disciples. To be sure, the Old Testament ceremonial law is fulfilled in a different way as the New Testament subsequently makes plain. But He begins explicitly to teach that His disciples are to continue to live under the authority of God's written revelation in the Old Testament.

At the end of the Sermon on the Mount, Jesus told His disciples the parable of the wise man and the foolish man. The wise man, He said, hears His words and obeys the teaching, but the foolish man hears His words and does not obey. When Jesus completed His teaching, including that parable, "the crowds were astonished at His teaching, for He taught them as one who had authority" (Matt. 7:24, 26, 28–29).

Jesus brackets this block of teaching (Matt. 5–7) with an opening reference to the Old Testament and a concluding reference to His words (to which He expects obedience). He implies that His words are to be treated with authority equal to that of the Old Testament. As the living Word of God, He places His teaching on a par with the written Word of God already given to Israel. For us the implication is clear. The Word of God comes to all generations of believers in the Old and New Testaments as the basis of authority under which disciples place themselves.

No one can cultivate an intimate relationship with the Lord without living under the authority of His Word. He has made this a precondition of discipleship in every age. Living under His authority as expressed in His Word enables disciples to cultivate their relationship with Him, be shaped like Him in their character, and be trained for His service.

If one is to live under the authority of God, one must

listen to the Word of God. Thus the first discipline of discipleship must be daily time in the Bible so that God can speak His Word to the disciple and thereby the relationship between the two is cultivated.. A disciple's daily intake of the Word of God comes in a slightly different form from the way it was made known to the Twelve. They had been taught the Old Testament, and they had the living Word of Jesus in their presence. Both were important. Accordingly, significant time every day in the Word of God in both Testaments is an essential spiritual discipline if one is to be a disciple of the Lord in any age.

The Discipline of Scripture Memory

Related to the discipline of reading and studying the Word is that of Scripture memory. The clearest illustration of this comes in Matthew 4 just before Jesus calls His disciples. Here, in preparation for His ministry, Jesus goes into the wilderness to be tempted by Satan. While the disciples are not present for that experience, it is obvious that for their edification He shared it with them. He intends for them to understand not only that He could resist temptation, but for them also to learn the principles by which they will be able to do the same. The key rule is found in Jesus' use of relevant passages of Scripture (Matt. 4:4, 7, 10). Jesus cites portions of the Bible not by His supernatural power as the Son of God, but in His human nature as the Son of Man. Jesus' point is that the Word that fortified Him in His resistance of temptation is available to each one of us as we face the same experience and fight off the Devil. Otherwise, the account of Jesus' experience is of no practical value to us. What He is really doing is modeling for His disciples the importance of learning passages of Scripture to make them available for spiritual warfare in a sudden temptation crisis.

Throughout the rest of His ministry Jesus often quoted from the Old Testament. One of His purposes was to demonstrate the value of the discipline of Scripture memory for preaching and teaching. Scripture memory implants the mind of God into our minds. Then the Holy Spirit uses what we have hidden in our hearts to remind us of the principles He wants us to apply to life. This is learning to think as God thinks. We can have no deep understanding of the Word of God without serious study. But beyond study our memory work fixes Scripture in our minds and thus makes the Word available when the Spirit is ready to use it.

The Discipline of Fellowship

The third spiritual discipline appears in Jesus' relationship to His disciples from the earliest days of His ministry. Living in an intimate fellowship with other disciples is so central for Jesus that immediately after He starts His public ministry, He begins to gather some men together (Matt. 4:18–22; Mark 1:16–20). Fellowship is another means to accomplish God's objectives. The discipline of group interaction with like-minded disciples cannot be overemphasized.

Significantly, Jesus does not train disciples in isolation from one another. He does not spend time with one disciple on Monday, another on Tuesday, another on Wednesday, and so forth; but He trains them together. There are, to be sure, one-on-one conversations, and relationships are developed during their time together. Yet He trains them in a way that meets the deep need for close fellowship with a few other people; therefore, He draws them together in a small group.

This discipline, fellowship, is essential for implementing the life-to-life transference principle discussed earlier. Unless the disciple commits himself to spend time with a disciple-maker and a few other disciples, life-to-life sharing cannot take place. In a sense, commitment to this discipline makes possible much of what takes place in the whole experience of discipleship. Without it the process cannot work.

In His first major teaching to His disciples, Jesus sets before them the practice of certain other spiritual disciplines that He expects them to build into their lives. He warns the disciples about Pharisees who employ spiritual disciplines for the wrong reasons. "Beware of practicing your piety before men in order to seen by them; for then you will have no reward from your Father who is in heaven" (Matt. 6:1). When He talks about the practice of piety, the word He uses is δικαιοσύνη which means righteousness. Jesus then discusses cultivation of the particular habits for righteous living that relationship with the Lord requires. Many overlook the distinction Jesus makes. While He corrects the abuse of these habits, He fully expects His disciples to practice them.

The Discipline of Giving

The fourth spiritual discipline is that of giving (Matt. 6:2–4). Jesus' initial statement concerns giving alms, but His emphasis on the principle of giving has larger implications for His disciples. Jesus knows that Christians need to give in order tangibly to express their gratitude for God's many blessings. He knows that gratitude must cost something if it is to be genuine thankfulness.

Jesus' teaching about giving assumes that the principle of the tithe from the Old Testament is a settled issue. This explains why the New Testament speaks little about tithing; Jesus and the leaders of the New Testament church presuppose it. For example, in criticizing the Pharisees Jesus says, "You tithe mint and dill and cummin, and have neglected weightier matters of the law, justice and mercy and faith; these you ought to have done, *without neglecting the others*" (Matt. 23:23, emphasis mine). While He is concerned about major issues like justice, mercy, and faith, He expects His followers not to neglect matters such as the tithe. Certainly those under the New Covenant are not expected to give less to God than those under the Old! If anything, they might be expected to do more.

The spiritual significance of a tithe concerns first of all a tangible expression of thanks to God. Yet it leads to other lessons in spiritual development as well. A few people can give the minimal tenth of their income and not miss its impact on their lifestyle. For most, however, the tithe significantly influences the way they live. Tithing requires readjustment of the balance of their income. Giving forces them to seek God's mind regarding effective and responsible use of all their resources. In fact the tithe reminds disciples that God wants to be Lord over all the resources of His people.

Additional spiritual depth may come from the practice of tithing if the remaining ninety percent of a disciple's income is inadequate to cover his basic needs. Then he has the privilege of trusting the Lord to provide for his needs in ways beyond ordinary income. Basically it becomes a matter of faith. The question facing the disciple is whether the Lord provides for His people's needs if they walk in obedience regarding their giving. It is remarkable how many spiritual lessons are learned by a disciple through the handling of finances. Trusting God for provision in this area leads to major growth for the disciple and his family.

Finally, giving helps to keep disciples free from their possessions and reminds them that their first allegiance is to the Lord. Temptations regarding mammon are constant for every believer, which explains why Jesus went to some pains early with the Twelve to talk about their relationship to money (Matt. 6:19–34). Systematic giving reminds disciples that possessions are really not theirs but the Lord's. Disciples are to be free from the temptation to cling to money and the power it brings. God uses the tithe to support His work throughout the world, but disciples need to tithe for their own good, whether or not God needs the money for spiritual ministries in the world.

The Discipline of Prayer

Prayer, or verbal communication with God, is an indispensable part of a person-to-person relationship (Matt. 6:5–15). If men are to know God, they must hear from Him through His Word and must respond in prayer.

Jesus began by teaching His disciples to communicate with their Father their whole hearts and minds. During their years with Jesus they talked directly to Him, and thereby developed their relationship with Him. Through prayer this relationship continued after His Ascension, just as He had taught them to speak to the Father. In both cases they learned the secret of a vital fellowship and to live in the presence of God. No close relationship is possible without significant two-way communication.

Many think that because God knows all things prayer is unnecessary. If God knows what disciples need, why should they ask Him? The question assumes that the chief function of prayer is to ask God to meet our needs. While this is a legitimate part of prayer, it is not the most basic reason to pray. Disciples are to pray in order to develop a relationship with God. That relationship assumes communication and the sharing of mind to mind and heart to heart, whether or not requests are made. If the only reason people talk to other people is to make requests of them, few close relationships would develop. People communicate because they long for friendships and love relationships.

One of the implications of this is that one cannot be a disciple of Jesus without time spent talking to Him. This discipline is usually coupled with study of the Word of God; these two disciplines are the primary means of communication with God and are the basis of any serious devotional time. Without daily time to hear from and to share with God, one cannot be a true disciple of Jesus.

The Discipline of Fasting

Jesus' teaching on fasting closely follows His discourse on the importance of prayer (Matt. 6:16–18). Fasting is abstinence from food and sometimes drink for a designated period of time. Normally connected with prayer, fasting signifies the sacrificial giving up of certain essentials of life. The Scriptures indicate two reasons for this practice: first, fasting makes additional time available for prayer and study of God's Word; second, it demonstrates to God the disciple's serious intent regarding current prayer concerns. Since the human body is designed for regular intake of food, the physical and emotional sacrifice of abstinence confirms the earnestness of the disciple about the matter of prayer.

Many believe that fasting increases spiritual sensitivity. In addition to this, fasting also appears to yield a wide range of emotional and physical benefits. Regular fasting helps to keep the body under control so that the appetites do not dominate the disciple's life. It seems to have a tempering effect, particularly upon the appetites for food and sex. Both of these appetites are legitimate, of course, but both need to be kept under God's control. It may well be that regular fasting is a means God uses to assist us in this matter.

The Discipline of Public Worship

The last discipline that Jesus sets before His disciples early in His relationship with them is that of regular public worship. As Jesus begins His public ministry, Luke says, "He went into the synagogue, as his custom was, on the sabbath day" (4:16; cf. Mark 6:2). It is evident that His disciples followed Him in this practice (Mark 6:1–2).

Jesus knows the value of worshiping God with other believers. The small group fellowship is significant, but it is not a substitute for participation in a larger assembly. The great congregation provides opportunity for teaching, preaching, praise, and fellowship. When Christians meet with a larger group of people belonging to God, they are reminded of membership in a greater whole. Those who would be disciples of Jesus in any generation need to be part of biblically centered, weekly public worship. That worship may take various forms, but participation in that experience is one of the things Jesus modeled for His men.

The Practice of Spiritual Disciplines

While this list of spiritual disciplines does not include all habit patterns that might assist in a disciple's spiritual growth, Jesus apparently considered these to be among the most essential. Spiritual disciplines were often the subject of His conversations and Jesus modeled them for His disciples from

His earliest days with them. Disciples in any age must commit themselves to building these patterns into their lives.

Any serious discussion of spiritual disciplines may lead some to ask, "Cannot disciplined habits simply lead to a legalism that implies keeping to these practices without enjoying the vital spirituality they were designed to produce?" The answer of course is yes; these certainly may lead to only the form of godliness. If practiced for the wrong reasons and/or without the empowering of the Holy Spirit of grace, they may become external exercises and in fact not accomplish their intended purpose at all. Jesus deals with this kind of problem when He discusses the Pharisees' abuses (Matt. 6). They were using these spiritual exercises for the wrong reasons, but Jesus' response is that His disciples are to use them rightly. According to Jesus, abuse did not justify abandoning the practices. The disciples were directed to restore these habit patterns to their original purpose as aids toward spiritual growth.

The principle Christ emphasized is that while spiritual disciplines may be profitless for those with wrong attitudes or motives, one cannot grow spiritually without using them. One may use them wrongly, but to neglect them is to forfeit the right to be a disciple of Jesus.

Other generations have helped keep these spiritual disciplines in perspective by referring to them as "means of grace." The phrase is a reminder that these holy patterns are not ends in themselves but are means of cultivating relationship with God. Ends and means go together but must not be confused. Disciples are not to practice these disciplines as ends in themselves. They are to use them as instruments that assist them to know God, allow Him to shape their character, and train them for ministry. Properly used, they are in a real sense the *means* of grace, God's way of working in the lives of His disciples.

THE PRINCIPLE OF ACCOUNTABILITY

Accountability is crucial for any kind of serious training and discipline. Disciples are to account for themselves.

Accountability to Jesus

The Twelve are accountable to Jesus for almost every aspect of their lives inasmuch as they move in His immediate presence all the time. He has opportunity to observe everything they do from their rising in the morning until they retire at night. He observes their actions, attitudes, interpersonal relationships, spiritual growth, and developing skills in ministry. He checks up on them when they return from missions on which He sends them (Mark 6:7–13, 30; Luke 9:1–6, 10). As part of life-to-life transference, they live and work together while Jesus holds them to account. Another reason, then, for the discipline of membership in a small fellowship is that the group serves as a vehicle for accountability. Those not committed to such a fellowship cannot be held accountable.

The disciples are also accountable to each other. When assigned to training missions, Jesus sends them two by two. Part of the reason for ministry teams is fellowship and encouragement, but another part is accountability. No disciple is completely on his own, but is responsible to a larger group committed to the same purposes. The disciples learn this principle so well that almost never does a lone spiritual leader appear in the New Testament church. With the exception of Philip (Acts 8) and Barnabas (Acts 11) for brief periods of time, spiritual leaders are always found in groups of two or more. That the apostles passed on this practice is evidenced by Barnabas and Paul who return regularly to give an account to the church at Antioch that had sent them out on their journeys.

Reason for Accountability

Accountability is essential because mankind is fallen. Sin has affected human motives and desires. As a result, Christians need to be accountable to other believers in order to help them do what they really desire to do and that which they know God desires them to do. Being accountable means that members of the body of Christ care enough for one another to hold each other responsible for practices which result in 1) a developing relationship with God, 2) growth in His likeness, and 3) accomplishment of His work in the world.

Accountability is usually the key factor in any consistent practice of spiritual disciplines. Most disciples know that they need to build spiritual habits into their lives. Weekly reporting of their faithfulness in the use of the means of grace remarkably affects disciples in the ordering of their lives. Many who never were able to get consistency in devotional practices find that rendering account builds patterns into their lives that previously had been difficult if not impossible for them.

Two Types of Accountability

There are two kinds of accountability. One is judgmental and tends to be strict and impersonal while focusing primarily upon performance. The other is supportive and challenging. The latter is more like the New Testament model that was designed to encourage and build up those seeking to be disciples. This pattern holds people accountable so that they may grow by discipline. Its purposes are educational and transformational. It is concerned about performance, but also takes into account motives of the heart and external circumstances. A supportive accountability cannot be lenient if it is to be genuine accountability. Further, it must include an element of discipline. At the same time, it asserts that disciplines are only means to ends and not ends in themselves. This kind of accountability works in every age because of the basic psychological and spiritual needs of human beings. Everyone needs praise and encouragement as complements to necessary correction and admonition. People must be affirmed as well as rebuked.

Three Basic Principles

Accountability seems to be the linchpin that holds together the commitment to spiritual disciplines with the principle of life-to-life transference. Those who share their lives with others have earned the right to hold them accountable. Further, only where accountability is operative do many become consistent in developing spiritual habits of the means of grace. In contemporary discipleship, weekly accountability to the disciplemaker and the entire group regarding the state of one's spiritual life and the use of spiritual disciplines is an essential minimum. Consequently, only through answering to others will genuine spiritual growth take place.

These three basic principles of discipleship are God's design for His grace to help His people grow as He desires. The combined principles of life-to-life transference, spiritual disciplines, and accountability form a spiritual life-support system for disciples. They are interdependent and essential if vital spirituality is to thrive. They are like a spiritual life-support system in that a disiciple cannot simply employ these for training for a brief period of time and then outgrow them. Rather, they are essential permanent ingredients in the life of everyone seeking to follow the Lord. At a certain level of maturity one may draw less upon the lives of leaders for spiritual food but will continue to draw on peers. A disciple always needs to share the lives of others; must employ the means of grace to cultivate his relationship with the Lord; and must seek the discipline of accountability. The mature, godly spiritual leaders whom God has used from New Testament times to the present have found practical ways to build all of these elements into their own lives throughout their lifetimes.

5

a training mission
for the twelve

JESUS' METHODS FOR MINISTRY:
AN OVERVIEW

The New Testament picture of Jesus' ministry begins with a capsule introduction to His message (Matt. 4:17), and then introduces His twofold method of ministry. The first part of this method is the calling of certain disciples around Himself for intense spiritual training (Matt. 4:18–22); the second part is His teaching, preaching, and healing ministry to larger groups. Thus Matthew portrays Jesus' ministry as having two major dimensions, each a deliberate part of His plan. Accordingly, Jesus has a private, concentrated ministry of discipleship with a few and a public ministry to many. Sometimes these larger groups were "multitudes." Throughout the Gospels both of these approaches are woven together. A significant amount of the Gospel materials is given to Jesus' public ministry and teaching, but even during these times the disciples are always present and in training in the midst of His public ministry. In fact, public ministry is often a training ground for more private ministry.

The significance for us of Jesus' dual method is, first, the disciples' involvement in both public and private ministry. He models for future disciples a ministry to large numbers of people while at the same time making disciples of a few.

Second, disciplemaking for the purpose of accomplishing His mission was His plan from the beginning, not an afterthought rising from a concern that his own life and ministry were in danger. This emphasis strongly implies that if Jesus is deliberate about this pattern for spiritual growth and leadership development, those following Him in future generations must be just as deliberate about the process of making disciples. Too often service for God is thought of only in terms of public ministry. Though that should not be minimized, an urgent need continues today for discipleship training to complement it.

JESUS TRAINS BY TEACHING AND ACTIVE MINISTRY

In Matthew 5–7 Jesus gives to the Twelve the essential content and meaning of the New Covenant. While others may have listened to His teaching, He intends this significant block of teaching for those who are going to be His disciplined followers. Here He deals with the major themes of character, service, righteousness, love, spiritual disciplines, personal finances, interpersonal relationships, trust in God, spiritual discernment, and obedience. Everyone desiring to be a disciple of Jesus must understand these key areas.

This teaching is followed in Matthew 8 and 9 by events that focus on His public ministry of healing, casting out of demons, and forgiving sins. But His private ministry with only a few followers also emerges in these materials in such events as the healing of Peter's mother-in-law (8:14–17), His dealing with impulsive and reluctant followers (8:18–22), the stilling of the storm (8:23–27), the call of Matthew (9:9–13), and questions about fasting that concerned both John's disciples and His own (9:14–17). These chapters demonstrate the interwoven public and private ministry activity of Jesus.

At the close of Matthew 9 the twofold focus of the ministry again comes into view. In 9:35 a capsule summary of the public ministry of Jesus appears, reminiscent of 4:23—

"Jesus went about all the cities and villages, teaching in their synagogues and preaching the gospel of the kingdom, and healing every disease and every infirmity." These two verses neatly bracket this entire section. As in chapter 4 where a picture of His discipleship ministry precedes the summary of His public ministry, so in chapter 9 following the summary of His public ministry, there is again a focus on the training of the Twelve. Jesus meets the needs of a sizeable group in His public activity, while at the same time investing Himself privately in a few lives.

A VISION OF THE PROBLEM: PEOPLE'S NEEDS

In Matthew 4–9 the disciples have had opportunity both to be taught by Jesus and to experience ministry under Him. They now know what He does for others, and they begin to know Him at a deeper level. By 9:36 they have discovered His compassionate heart for the spiritually leaderless multitudes. "When He saw the crowds, He had compassion on them, because they were harassed and helpless, like sheep without a shepherd." People are adrift, surrounded with difficulties and problems their own resources cannot meet. Thus, the disciples begin to see people as Jesus sees them and to discover His heart for those in need. They are beginning to catch a vision of the problem as Jesus views it.

Jesus is now able to clarify the difficulty of the problem that they face. "Then He said to His disciples, 'The harvest is plentiful, but the laborers · are few'" (Matt. 9:37). The problem is that the harvest of needs is so great while the people to meet those needs are so few. Instead of just telling His disciples of the great needs, He allows them to live with Him for a long enough period of time that they can see firsthand just how many people are in need. This is the first half of the problem.

JESUS IMPARTS A VISION OF THE PROBLEM: TOO FEW WORKERS

Jesus wants His disciples to see more than the magnitude of the needs, however; He wants them to understand the solution to those needs. The problem is not just the plentiful harvest, but the absence of laborers for the harvest. The solution must lie with the laborers and shepherds, and far too few of those are available to meet people's needs. Jesus wants His disciples to see that even the Son of God cannot meet all the needs of people in His own day. Even Jesus with his miracle-working power is unable, because of the limits of time and energy, to deal with all the spiritual, physical, and emotional problems of people. The disciples are beginning to glimpse the fact that Jesus cannot do this work alone. In spite of the tremendous public ministry, the task is overwhelming.

Jesus has allowed the disciples to see and experience the problem of every spiritual leader in any age, that there is too much ministry to be done for too many people by too few laborers. This creates a danger that the work will not get done at all and, consequently, that people's needs will not be met. Furthermore, there is the danger of overloading the too few laborers who are available and wearing them out prematurely.

JESUS PROVIDES THE SOLUTION

Prayer

Jesus has a twofold solution to this problem. First, He exhorts His disciples to pray to the Lord of the harvest. Prayer is a reminder of the disciples' dependence on God for His solutions as well as His grace to carry them out. The work of ministry is not going to be adequately carried forward unless it is soaked in prayer. Here the focus of prayer is not the harvest, but for God to send laborers into His harvest (Matt. 9:38). Though only laborers in training, it is the disciples' responsibility to pray that the Lord will increase the number of people whom He is sending to do His ministry. Prayer for additional laborers is a priority for every work of God.

Training Disciples

The second part of Jesus' solution addresses the problem of an inadequate labor force. He has already begun to deal with that by gathering disciples to Himself and training them. A further step in that process appears as He calls the disciples to Him, gives them authority, and sends them out to minister (Matt. 10:1, 5). This is always God's solution to the problem of meeting people's needs: training others to minister to His people.

THE HEART OF THE SOLUTION: MULTIPLICATION

At the heart of Jesus' solution is the principle of multiplication. It is clear to Jesus, and now to His disciples, that even one with supernatural capacities cannot meet all the human needs around Him. But through the principles of discipleship, Jesus multiplies Himself by twelve and so begins to do twelve times the ministry that He did alone. Since training the disciples involves such a significant portion of His time and energy, a certain amount of Jesus' public ministry must be reduced. He is not able to do all He might if He were using all of His personal resources in the public arena. He thinks strategically and realizes that less time in public ministry is essential so that He can invest time in the concentrated ministry of disciplemaking. Ultimately this will mean a far greater public ministry because of multiplication.

The implication for spiritual leaders is clear. Leaders cannot invest all their energy and time in public ministry. They must be involved in discipleship training if all the needed ministry is to be accomplished. Making disciples is not an optional extra in ministry; it cannot be neglected without seriously undermining all the public ministry necessary to meet the needs of people.

The multiplication process is apparent in the Gospels. Not only does Jesus multiply Himself by twelve, but in Luke 10 He multiplies Himself by 70. Luke is the only author to describe the mission of the Seventy, but it is difficult to escape the observation that the instructions and the training for the Seventy in Luke 10 are almost identical to that of the Twelve in Matthew 10. Where did the Seventy come from? While the Scriptures are not explicit about this, they seem to imply that workers were brought into some kind of relationship with Jesus through the Twelve. It had happened that way with some of the disciples.

Thus Andrew brought Peter to Jesus, as we have seen, and probably John brought his brother James. Philip enrolled Nathanael, and it is not accidental that Philip came from the same city as Andrew and Peter (John 1:41–44). If such a pattern continued, very likely the Twelve each brought five or six people to Jesus and perhaps were used by Him to assist in their training. With the multiplication principle at work, the men, each investing himself in five or six others, have now multiplied the public ministry. Now seventy are in God's harvest.

If the Seventy could only catch the vision for the public ministry and also understand the principle of multiplying themselves in a few other disciples, the process would continue. If each of the Seventy were to disciple five others, an additional 350 people would be involved in ministry. If the 350 each discipled five others, the next disciple generation would include still another 1,750 involved in public ministry. While there is no way to know for certain that the Seventy and those who followed them understood perfectly the pattern set before them, the hypothesis illustrates that the principle of multiplication within four disciple generations would produce over 2,000 people involved in spiritual ministry for God $(1 + 12 + 70 + 350 + 1,750)$. These figures demonstrate that the principle of multiplication has built into it a factor of geometric progression. This involves not only adding a few other disciples but multiplying disciplemakers.

It is this multiplication factor that may account for the enormous growth of the church in its first two centuries. It also reminds observers that this is God's method for touching

His world in any generation. No spiritual leader or group of leaders, even with the aid of media technology, can reach the world for Christ or meet all the needs of people. The only hope of doing what God wants done in the world is to use His method of making disciples and multiplying them in every generation.

PRINCIPLES OF DISCIPLESHIP TRAINING: THE PRIORITY OF BEING WITH JESUS

The picture of Jesus' sending out disciples on their first training mission in Matthew 10 provides a glimpse into key discipleship principles. Several reiterate previous lessons, but others are new principles Jesus is building into their lives. The opening verses of the chapter emphasize His order of priority for the Twelve. He calls them "to Him," and then the Twelve are sent out (Matt. 10:1, 5). First, the disciples cultivate their relationship with Jesus; only then are they to be used by Him in ministry. Mark emphasizes the same point in describing Jesus' appointment and choice of the Twelve "to be *with Him* and to be sent out to preach and to have authority" (Mark 3:14, emphasis mine). Jesus is concerned that the disciples learn to minister to other people, but it is to be *out of their personal relationship with Himself.* Despite other facets of the discipleship process, learning to be with Jesus is the top priority so that the resulting relationship may transform individuals and prepare them for service.

THE IMPORTANCE OF LIVING UNDER AUTHORITY

In preparing the Twelve for ministry, Jesus delegates to them certain authority, particularly in the areas of preaching and healing (Mark 3:14; Matt. 10:1). The principle of disciples living under the authority of the Lord is now extended as He gives them certain responsibilities. The implication is that disciples sent to minister for Jesus do so not on their own authority but by the authority of the Lord.

Their commission to and motive for ministry is not their own. It is given to them because of the One to whom they belong. Under authority themselves, they are given authority to represent the Lord and to do His ministry. The question of authority means that the disciples have an obligation to fulfill a responsibility assigned to them. Failure to fulfill their responsibility is disobedience to the Lord. The work they do carries with it an authority much greater than anything from within themselves. Therefore, they need not be self-conscious about fulfilling the assignment given to them.

THE SIGNIFICANCE OF CHOOSING A TARGET POPULATION

In sending out His disciples, Jesus gives them a specific target population. He instructs them not to go to Gentiles or Samaritans, but "to the lost sheep of the house of Israel" (Matt. 10:5–6). Later they will be given the responsibility of reaching out not only to Israel but to Samaria and all the nations of the earth (Matt. 28:19–20; Acts 1:8). But for this training mission, the group of people for whom they are responsible is narrow. The lesson for modern disciples is suggestive. If the target population is too broad, disciples tend to get torn too easily among the needs of various groups. It may be that this explains the divisions of responsibility among spiritual leaders in the early church. For example, men like Barnabas and Paul had a special role in ministry to the Gentiles.

This incident suggests that every disciple may need to ask the Lord for a definite vision for a specific group of people. The needy people of the world may be divided by geography, language, culture, education, type of work, age, and so forth. Not every disciple is responsible in the same way for every single people group in the world. One task of every disciple will be to discern what is God's specific direction about the group of people for whom he or she is to carry special responsibility at any designated time.

THE DISCIPLES' TRAINING FOR MINISTRY

The disciples' public ministry activity on their mission is significant. They are specifically instructed to preach and exercise caring ministries (such as healing the sick, raising the dead, cleansing lepers, and casting out demons) as a part of their task (Matt. 10:7–8). In giving an account to Jesus of their activities upon their return, they also indicate that they had been involved in a teaching ministry (Mark 6:30). They know how to teach, preach, and heal because they had been with Jesus when He did those three kinds of ministry (Matt. 4:23; 9:35). They know what to do and how to do it because Jesus has been transferring his vision and purpose. They know what to say because they were with Jesus when He was "teaching in their synagogues and preaching the gospel of the kingdom" (Matt. 9:35) day after day, week after week. Through repetition the disciples gained a thorough understanding of what the kingdom of God is all about.

For modern disciples this means that Jesus also sets our forms of ministry. But it also implies that these forms are to be modeled before others by a disciplemaker. While Jesus proclaims the content necessary for meeting people's spiritual needs, the modern disciplemaker explains and applies it in a contemporary setting. What we are to do for God as well as what we are to say must be built on His Word, but at the same time it must be practically modeled in a contemporary discipleship setting.

THE DISCIPLES' TRAINING ABOUT MONEY AND MINISTRY

Jesus, in His instructions to His disciples, develops two principles regarding finance. The first principle results from the combination of two statements: "You receive without pay, give without pay," and "the laborer deserves his food" (Matt. 10:8, 10). Since both come from Jesus, one must not be interpreted in such a way as to make it contradict the other. When Jesus says that since they receive without pay, therefore they are to give without pay, He clearly cannot mean that they should never receive support from others for the basic necessities of life. The rest of New Testament teaching indicates that those who give full time to ministry deserve support by the body of believers. Those giving all their energies to ministry are to get their living from the gospel. The laborer does deserve his food.

But Jesus cautions His disciples that their motivation for ministry in making disciples is not to be financial. As they have been trained by Him without pay, they are to minister to others both publicly and privately in the same way, i.e., not on the basis of whether or not people assist them financially. Jesus indicates that their basic necessities will be provided for, but they are to guard their own motivation.

This is coupled with a second principle related to finance in Jesus' instructions. They are to "take no gold, nor silver, nor copper in [their] belts, nor bag for [their] journey, nor two tunics, nor sandals, nor staff" (Matt. 10:9–10). Disciples must learn to trust God to provide for their needs while they are in His service. It is a faith lesson. If they can learn it well during their training period, they can trust God whatever their financial state the rest of their lives. This accounts for Jesus' encouragement at the end of the gospel story to take along whatever resources they have at hand (Luke 22:35ff.). Having learned their lessons of dependence upon God to meet their needs, they now will be good stewards of the resources God has provided.

The two principles related to finance are complementary. Motivation for ministry and disciplemaking is not to be financial gain. Disciples must understand that God can take care of their needs in any circumstance. Some of the greatest spiritual growth takes place in settings that require trusting Him for finances or material needs which would not otherwise be supplied. Jesus wants His disciples to live so that they are free to trust God to meet all of their needs.

THE DISCIPLES' TRAINING IN STRATEGY FOR MINISTRY

The next lessons for the disciples are Jesus' specific instructions about going to a village, finding out who is worthy in that place, and staying in that house until ministry there is finished (Matt. 10:11–15). Jesus had several purposes in mind in these instructions. First, if the disciples find out who is worthy in any place, they also may well find those who are open to God and concerned for spiritual things. Second, the chance to stay in one home over a period of days provides opportunities for initial private or concentrated ministry with only a few people. The disciples will have more time with the head and other members of the household; therefore, they will be able to make a significant spiritual investment. Thus while they are involved in the public ministry of teaching, preaching, and healing, the disciples are also to look for opportunities for more concentrated time with at least one family in every village.

Third, that concentrated time, coupled with public ministry, will likely leave behind significant witness to the gospel. Fourth, failure to find someone willing to keep them in their home might indicate insufficient interest in spiritual things to make it worthwhile for the disciples to invest their time there. They are to go on to more responsive locations. He instructs the disciples to be discerning about people and their hunger for God, and to invest their time and energy accordingly.

THE DISCIPLES' TRAINING IN MEETING OPPOSITION

After giving them instructions on how to proceed, Jesus reminds His disciples that they will normally face opposition to the things of God. He describes them as sheep in the midst of wolves. He counsels them therefore to be as wise as serpents but innocent as doves (Matt. 10:16–23). Wisdom and integrity, He implies, are essential in the midst of a hostile environment. They are to beware of people and expect the kind of hostility that will place them in unusual situations, but they are to be ready to bear witness to Jesus in those circumstances. He tells them that it will not be they who are speaking in difficult situations, but that the Spirit of the Father will speak through them (Matt. 10:20). Disciples must be psychologically prepared for situations hostile to the gospel and the things of God. They need to be reminded of the promise of the presence of the Spirit to speak through them and, accordingly, enabling them to testify to Jesus appropriately.

Since not all hostility comes from the outside, Jesus warns that even their families may turn against them (Matt. 10:21–23). Opposition is expected from some quarters, but they must be aware that it sometimes comes from home. They must be prepared to persevere in the light of opposition from any source. Later the Twelve have opportunity to see Jesus handle opposition from His own family (Mark 3:21–35; John 7:3–8).

THE PURPOSE OF THE DISCIPLES' TRAINING: TO BE LIKE JESUS

After setting a number of instructions before His disciples, Jesus reminds them that "a disciple is not above his teacher, nor a servant above his master; it is enough for a disciple to be like his teacher and the servant to be like his master" (Matt. 10:24–25). Jesus is telling them that if He as their Teacher and Master is the object of persecution (ranging from religious authorities of His day to misunderstandings by His own family), they as His disciples should expect the same treatment. He continues to model before them the way in which one lives with opposition.

However, the disciples are to be like their Master in other ways as well. They are to be like Him in their ministry activities, i.e., teaching, preaching, and caring ministries. They are to be like Him in speaking about the kingdom of God. They are to be like Him in trusting God to supply their financial needs. They are to be like Him in ministering to large groups and to a few households in the beginning of a concentrated ministry. This is the purpose of life-to-life transference; the disciples are not only to learn from the Lord but ultimately are to be like Him in both character (as revealed in their attitudes and reactions to people) and actions (as revealed in their ministries).

THE COST OF DISCIPLESHIP

Then Jesus exhorts the men not to fear opposition, but to fear only any lack of faithfulness or failure on their part to testify for the Lord. They must not let opposition bring them to the place where they deny Jesus. "Do not fear those who can kill the body but cannot kill the soul; rather fear him who can destroy both soul and body in hell" (Matt. 10:28).

Finally, Jesus begins to specify the cost of being His disciple. Part of that cost is His insistence on being first in their lives. Consequently, He indicates to His disciples that sometimes a man will be set against his father, a daughter against her mother, a daughter-in-law against her mother-in-law. At least at times, He says, "A man's foes will be those of his own household" (Matt. 10:35–36). Jesus is looking for disciples who have made Him the first priority of their lives. "He who loves father or mother more than me is not worthy of me; and he who loves son or daughter more than me is not worthy of me" (Matt. 10:37). He wants His disciples to reach a point where He is more important to them than anyone else in the world. This is part of the cost of being all that Jesus desires a disciple to be (cf. Luke 14:26).

But Jesus is not content just with the disciples' willingness to make Him more important than their families. He wants to be more important than their very lives. "He who does not take up His cross and follow me is not worthy of me. He who finds his life will lose it, He who loses his life for my sake will find it" (Matt. 10:38–39). The reference to taking up the cross is a challenge to be willing to die for Jesus. It is the first indication in the Gospels of the importance the Cross will assume. Jesus tries to prepare His followers for the ultimate price they may have to pay for discipleship, namely to lay down their lives for Him (cf. Luke 14:27).

Implications of the cost of discipleship for contemporary disciples are twofold. First, disciples must come to the place where Jesus is the most important person in their lives. Second, they must learn that following Him in obedience is more important than preserving their own lives. The disciples of Jesus did not learn these lessons quickly or easily, but they did learn them. And His desire is the same for all those who would be His disciples.

DISCIPLESHIP TRAINING AND PUBLIC MINISTRY

When Jesus finished instructing His disciples, "He went on from there to teach and preach in their cities" (Matt. 11:1). While He trains the Twelve He continues His own public ministry of teaching, preaching, and healing. To train disciples does not mean one forfeits one's public responsibilities. Further, it seems that Jesus actually follows His disciples to complement the ministry they have had in various places. They may in fact be preparing the way for His more effective ministry. This would especially be the case if by the reference to "their cities" Matthew means that Jesus went particularly to the cities from which His disciples had come. Further, if He had sent each of them to his home area, that might account for the explicit warnings in His instructions about opposition from their families. Jesus might also be strategically visiting places where they would have natural contacts with people seriously interested in spiritual things. Jesus then would be following them to build on their relationships and the ministry they had developed ahead of Him.

The application of these principles in discipleship today means several things. The first is that spiritual leadership does not need to set aside public ministry in order to make disciples. The two are best done simultaneously so that those in training will learn from the public ministry of a disciplemaker. The call to make disciples is a call to add an activity that will multiply an already existing ministry. Many who have effective public ministries to sizeable groups of people must learn the value of multiplying that ability for the body of Christ through the making of disciples.

The second implication is that disciplemakers must learn to design public ministry as a complement to discipleship and vice versa. Those training disciples must find ways to complement the efforts of disciples they are training, while at the same time designing ministry for disciples that will complement their own ministry to other people.

The third implication is that many times disciples-in-training should be sent to their home areas to serve. They need to cultivate contacts through family and friendship evangelism. If making disciples is built around cultivating existing relationships, then that is the natural place to begin. Usually the closest ones are family and good friends. These must be developed for the sake of the gospel and the sake of the disciple's growth in effective ministry.

The training mission for the Twelve is described in detail in Matthew 10. The fact that explicit instructions are given regarding their mission is indicative of how important these basic principles are for every disciple. They are given to show the basic principles and methods of discipleship training as well as many of the primary lessons that a disciple needs to learn during training. While the lessons had a specific application for the Twelve under Jesus' direction, the principles involved are applicable in every age and culture. These must be taken seriously if disciples are actually made in the way in which Jesus made them.

6

servant disciples

JESUS' PURPOSES

The concept of discipleship begins with the picture of a holy God looking for a holy people. Thus God not only says that He is holy, He defines holiness in terms of righteousness and love. At Sinai He begins to form a people around Himself who are to reflect His holy character in both righteousness and love (Ex. 20; Lev. 19). This pattern is paralleled when Jesus draws the new Israel of God around Himself and begins to impart His holiness to the disciples. After they begin to follow Him, He gives them the standard of righteousness and love reflected in His own nature (Matt. 5). His major concern is their being, i.e., what they are; so He focuses upon character.

Yet Jesus is interested in more than character; He is concerned also about service, i.e., what the disciples are to do with their lives. So at the end of His three-year investment in the men, during that final full evening of fellowship and instruction with them recorded in John 13–17, He explains more specifically their call and task. It is on a Thursday night that Jesus gathers the Twelve in the Upper Room for what He knows will be the last opportunity for input into their lives. The occasion is particularly significant for our understanding of discipleship, and it explains why John gives it the attention he does. Five out of twenty-one chapters are devoted to it. For three years Jesus' two concerns have been to mold character into the likeness of God and to prepare the men for a lifetime of service. It is not surprising that on His last night with His men He focuses on them again.

LIFE WORK AS A SERVANT

The Scriptures describe ministry in a number of ways. God talked about a kingdom of priests at the founding of the nation (Ex. 19). Jesus calls persons to be fishers of men, salt, and light (Matt. 4:19; 5:13–14). He tells His men He wants them to be disciplemakers (Matt. 28). In John 13, this lifework for the disciples is described in terms of servanthood. God looks for people to give themselves to Him so fully that their lifework is to serve Him. Whatever they do, He wants to be the Master in charge.

Jesus embodies, and models, that servant role for the Twelve. Thus, in the middle of their meal together, He takes off His outer garment, pours a basin of water, wraps Himself with a towel, and begins to wash the disciples' feet as evidence that He is willing to serve and to give of Himself. This familiar story must be read thoughtfully, for it symbolizes everything Jesus has been doing for the Twelve. He says, "You call me Teacher and Lord; and you are right." As Teacher and Lord Jesus has given of Himself. If He does this out of His position of authority in their lives, the disciples must do the same for others. The story also reemphasizes the pouring out of His life for three years in the company of these men. This is just one more concrete expression of Jesus' servantlike attitude as He invested Himself in them.

THE SERVANT AND LOVE

This is not an isolated instance. It represents His gift of Himself to train the Twelve in what they are to be and do. His servanthood is wrapped up in the whole process of making them into disciples; it is the essence of life-to-life sharing. Jesus has invested in them, and as He finishes He says to them, "A new commandment I give to you, that you love one another; even as I have loved you, that you also love one another" (John 13:34). Loving is not the new element, for earlier they had been directed to love (Lev. 19:18, 34). Now they are called to love as Jesus loves them, pouring His life into them as disciplemaker. It has been life-to-life, heart-to-heart, day after day. Jesus comes to the end of His time with them and says in effect, "Now go and do in each other's life what I have been doing for you. Go and invest in each other, strengthen each other, build each other up and train each other."

He implies that they are to extend the process as well to others beyond their small circle. This is part of multiplying disciples. Later they will be commanded to make disciples of all nations. One of the ways they are to love one another as Jesus loved them is by giving their lives for each other and pouring out their lives for one another. Thus a commitment to the principles of discipleship is right at the heart of what Jesus' life was about. He calls them to the same task. If the Great Commission is in fact for every age, then He still seeks those who are willing to be disciples and, ultimately, to participate in making other disciples.

THE PROBLEM OF THE SERVANT

At this point, the disciples plainly are not quite where Jesus wants them to be. They have not, for example, washed one another's feet. They are each waiting for someone else to act. Since there is no servant to do it and none of them is willing to serve the others, they finally start to eat. Why are they unwilling to serve one another? The reason, quite simply, is pride in their hearts. None wants to take the lowest place. The questions that still concern them are "who is the greatest in the kingdom?" and "who will sit on the right hand and who on the left?" Since nobody wants to become last in line nor the first to surrender authority and influence, none takes the lowly task of a servant. Self-centeredness and pride still remain despite the maturing of character that has taken place over three years. Something else is still needed.

THE SERVANT AND SUBMISSION

Jesus is concerned about His disciples' lifework, but He is also concerned about their character. He began the discipleship process by telling them the kind of character He desires (Matt. 5–7). He now returns to deal with this central matter. He is looking for servants with special qualities, servants who are like the holy God who reveals Himself in righteousness and love.

On this last night Jesus addresses the central issue of the disciples' surrender of themselves as servants of the Lord. Recall that God has revealed that one aspect of His holy character is righteousness. If people are to be made holy, a proper expression of that holiness will be obedience to God's standard of righteousness and a willingness to obey God and His Word. Submission to the will of God means obedience to the Word of God. This explains Jesus' use of the images of the master and the slave, the owner and the servant. This metaphor was pertinent in the Roman Empire where so many owned slaves. Whatever the master asked, the servant performed so that the will of the master became in practice the will of the servant. Jesus asks for them to be totally submissive to the will of God as their Master/Owner. They are to be servants, slaves, who will instantly obey the will of the One to whom they belong.

THE MODEL OF THE SERVANT

Jesus is not satisfied for them simply to understand this figure rationally. He gives them a practical model of the kind of servant for whom He was looking. He Himself as the servant of God in full submission to God's will for His life is the example. As He says in the final verses of John 12, "I have not spoken on my own authority; the Father who sent me has Himself given me commandment what to say and what to speak . . . What I say, therefore, I say as the Father has bidden me" (vv. 49–50). Jesus is not speaking casually. He Himself is under the authority of God the Father and is submissive to His will.

In Gethsemane on this very same night, we may observe the most graphic picture of Jesus in perfect submission to the will of His Father. He has met with His men, now He takes them to the Garden and begins to pray in agony, "Father, is there any other way to accomplish the redemption of the world but this? If possible let this cup pass from me; nevertheless, not my will but yours be done." In this unique event He gives them once again a portrait of what He wants in a servant, i.e., one totally submissive to the whole will of God.

Where are the disciples in the process of becoming this kind of servant? How close are they to living in this same state of surrender to the full will of God? John 13 shows two examples of disciples dealing with the issue, the submission of their wills to the Lord. Of course already they have been partially submissive or they would not have been disciples for three years. They have been under Jesus' influence and walked with Him. But Jesus looks for something more, a total submission representing a choice of full obedience.

ONE SERVANT REFUSES SUBMISSION

One of the disciples dealing with this issue is Judas. No one knows all of Judas' reasons for his betrayal of the Lord. Perhaps he wanted the money and was greedy, or was just deluded in his own thinking with regard to what needed to be done. Maybe he thought he could precipitate a crisis in Jesus' life by forcing His hand, causing Him to rise up with his followers to throw off the yoke of Rome. But the heart of the matter is Judas' decision to do things his way instead of the Lord's. In refusing to submit to the way God wants to do things, he takes himself out of a right relationship with Jesus and ultimately destroys himself. Unsubmissive disciples may not lose that relationship with Jesus altogether. Yet Judas' example shows that it can happen. In this case it comes at the point of His unwillingness to submit his will and his life to Jesus as complete Master. The consequences of Judas' refusal of submissive servanthood are enormous.

ANOTHER SERVANT CHOOSES SUBMISSION

The other disciple facing the issue of submission to authority is Peter. As Jesus washes the feet of those around the circle, Peter is horrified. The closer Jesus gets to him the more uncomfortable he feels, perhaps because he was responsible for arrangements for the feast. Certainly he is embarrassed that Jesus is doing this when he knows somebody else should be. So when Jesus comes to him, he refuses to allow his feet to be washed. However, when Jesus confronts him, Peter yields. He wants the Lord's way and cries out, "Lord not only my feet but my hands and my head." Before the evening is over, it is obvious that Peter's submission is incomplete. Yet he is moving in the right direction. It is just this for which Jesus is looking: a willingness to submit life and character to Him.

THE SERVANT AND LOVE

Jesus not only desires a servant yielded to His control, and therefore living righteously, but one who reflects His character in love. Both the Father and Son make clear that a holy God reveals Himself not only by His standard of righteousness but in a loving heart. Jesus is looking for followers who are obedient to God's standard, submissive to His authority, and who will love as He loves. The centrality of this agape love is expressed in the fact that John 13 is bracketed by references to love in verse 1 and verses 34–35. Through this event Jesus models the kind of holy love He wants to see in His disciples' lives. The model is apparent both in His teaching and in His life. John introduces the narrative of the events of this last evening with the statement, "When Jesus knew that His hour had come to depart out of the world to the Father, having loved His own who were with Him in the world, He loved them to the end." That means all twelve of them. John focuses on the concrete example of this love: He "began to wash the disciples' feet," everyone's feet—including Judas'. Although Jesus knows Judas' heart and is aware of his plans, He loves him unconditionally and expresses that love in self-giving service.

This final night expresses the standard of love Jesus described for them in Matthew 5. "You have heard that it was said, You shall love your neighbor and hate your enemy. But I say to you, Love your enemies and pray for those who persecute you" (Matt. 5:43–44). Now Jesus has a chance to take His own teaching seriously, i.e., to love someone who is becoming a persecuting enemy. But Jesus does it. He gives the men a chance to see what that full love, that perfect love that He described in Matthew 5, is like in real life. In spite of knowing what Judas will do to Him, He keeps on loving him. Judas does not respond. In spite of all Jesus does for Him, in spite of all the love of God flowing to him through the person of Jesus, and in spite of all his privileges and opportunities, Judas turns his back and goes his own way. Even when Judas rejects Him, Jesus does not stop loving him. It is a graphic illustration of the unconditional, sacrificial love of God.

THE OBJECTS OF SERVANT LOVE

The kind of love that Jesus talks about and models before the Twelve expresses the holiness of God, and it has two objects. It is first directed toward God the Father, and then toward men and women. Jesus wants His disciples to learn to love God and to love others with an unconditional, unselfish kind of love. He wants them to be able to love their enemies, even one who has lived in their midst and seems to be their friend, yet now has revealed himself as their enemy. So he says to them, "Love one another even as I have loved you." Loving others, however, is second. First is loving God with the whole heart. In fact, that kind of love for God makes it possible to love people unconditionally as Jesus does. Jesus has modeled precisely this truth for three years before them.

His disciples do love the Father and love the Son, but Jesus has not finished with their love yet. An appendix to the chapter appears right after this discussion about the way Jesus loves them and how they are to love one another and about the whole example of unselfish, self-giving love. Here Peter asks Jesus where He is going. Jesus says, "Where I am going you cannot follow, but you shall follow afterward." Peter responds, "Why cannot I follow you now? I will lay down my life for you." Here is a picture of one man telling another that he loves Him and is committing his life to Him. But Jesus knows Peter's heart better than Peter himself does. He says to Peter that before the night is over Peter will deny Him three times.

Unquestionably, Peter loves Jesus, but his love is not yet perfect, not complete. He still loves his own life and himself to the extent that later he will flee from the garden and deny his Lord in the courtyard of the high priest. Peter loves Him but not yet fully as Jesus wants him to love. This explains why Jesus will draw Peter aside after the resurrection and ask, "Peter, do you love me more than these?" (John 21:15–17). For that is what He desires to see in Peter. He longs for Peter to love Him more than anything else in the world. His desire is the same for every disciple.

THE KEY TO SERVANT DISCIPLESHIP: THE HOLY SPIRIT

Jesus still seeks servant disciples, disciples wholly submitted to His will as a slave to a master. But He also desires that they have a heart of love like God's. It is no accident that this event in John 13 introduces an evening of teaching in which Jesus begins to explain the full implications of what is about to happen. His goal is to prepare His disciples for the more complete work of the Holy Spirit in their lives. It is in that crucial teaching time which is recorded in John 14–16 that the great truths about the Spirit and His coming are explained. Jesus is getting the disciples ready for what the Holy Spirit will do in them. This means that John has, in chapter 13, given the picture of the problem Jesus still sees in their lives. He follows with the solution that Jesus began to lay before them in John 14–16, namely, Jesus' most nearly complete teaching on the person and work of the Holy Spirit.

Jesus would like to do the same kind of work in all disciples through the power of the fullness of the Spirit. He longs to transform them to be like Himself, fully submissive to the whole will of God and loving as He loved. And He can if they will do two things. First, by an act of the will they must lay their lives before Him and submit themselves to Him, offering themselves as slaves to a master. Second, they must at the same time choose to love as He loves. The choice by itself does not change a disciple's heart. Yet it does makes possible that change, for when by faith those choices are made for God, His supernatural grace transforms the inner character of the heart. The disciple can then become like the Lord, holy as He is holy. God works through the power of the Holy Spirit as He takes total control and works out His full will and character in each disciple.

7

the commission to make disciples

The final picture that Matthew's Gospel gives us of Jesus is the story of the Lord's life assignment to His disciples. We usually refer to this as the Great Commission. The Twelve experienced three years of living together in the discipleship process and, in recent weeks, they witnessed the traumatic scenes of the Cross and the Resurrection. In the final resurrection appearance recorded by Matthew, Jesus meets His disciples, now reduced to eleven, on a mountain in Galilee where they worship Him. They still have questions, but they are there because they belong to Him.

LIVING IN FAITH

This episode reiterates several of the lessons Jesus has spent months building into the disciples. It highlights their personal relationship to Him, noting their devotion so that "when they saw Him, they worshipped Him" (Matt. 28:17). Their intimate relationship with Him is built upon faith: they believe in Him. Now that they know He is alive forever, they worship Him with a deeper understanding of His divine nature than they ever had before. They began as men of faith, but now their faith reaches an entirely different level. It will continue to bind them to the personal presence of Jesus the rest of their lives. Further, this faith is at the heart of their response to the promise Jesus gave to them, "I am with you always, till the close of the age" (Matt. 28:20).

LIVING UNDER AUTHORITY

Notice two matters that come out of their relationship with Jesus. First, they are clearly still under the authority of the Lord. When Jesus directs them to a mountain in Galilee, in obedience they go. Second, they may obey confidently because their ministries will be backed by "all authority in heaven and earth" which the Father has turned over to their Master (Matt. 28:18). The declaration of His authority is made to His disciples and to all others who will become disciples through the ages. That authority is the basis for going to make disciples of all nations.

Because Jesus has authority from the Father, He sends His disciples to make other disciples. This means that any disciple of Jesus, living under His authority, must be involved in some significant way in making other disciples. Being a disciple clearly leads to making other disciples. The choice to begin making disciples does not come from the desires of the Eleven, from an appreciation of their training, or from the wishes of would-be disciples. They are to become disciple-makers simply because Jesus commanded it. Failure to do what He has instructed is disobedience. Involvement in the process of disciplemaking is not an option for those who are Jesus' disciples.

LIVING IN FELLOWSHIP

While they are still under the authority of the Lord, they are also committed to each other. They gather in Galilee, and when Jesus commands them to make disciples, He speaks in the second person plural: You all go, make disciples together. From the account of their activity in Acts, they evidently understood this fully—that they are to continue in fellowship with one another and serve together in the making of other disciples. A bonding has taken place among the men as well as to Jesus, and now they go forth together in ministry to do His will.

THE HEART OF THE GREAT COMMISSION

The Great Commission forms a dramatic close to Matthew's Gospel. After investing His life for three years in disciples, Jesus now instructs them to go forth and make other disciples. It is as though Matthew is trying to help us understand that the disciples saw this as their life assignment from Jesus after three significant years of preparation.

Jesus delcares His will to the Eleven, "Go therefore and make disciples of all nations, baptizing them in the name of the Father, and the Son and the Holy Spirit, teaching them to observe all that I have commanded you" (Matt. 28:19–20). The central focus of the Commission, actually somewhat obscure in English, is much clearer in Greek. Jesus' statement has one main verb, and it is in the imperative: "make disciples." Three participles are related to the verb: "going," "baptizing," and "teaching." The participial instructions are subordinate to the main verb "make disciples." The focus, then, is not so much on going to all nations, or on baptizing or teaching; it is upon the making of disciples. Some older translations had the Great Commission focus upon "teaching all nations," but this distorts the central focus of what Jesus says. Teaching is included in making disciples, but it is a subordinate element.

Jesus' command to go and make disciples does not include detailed instructions about methods. Clearly, however, they know what to do because of Jesus' work in their lives. They can make disciples because they have been made into disciples. Jesus essentially says to them, "You go and do in others' lives what I have done in yours." The disciples know this process will include the essential ingredients of life-to-life investment, training believers in the use of primary spiritual disciplines, and the principle of accountability to help newer followers of Jesus build a spiritual life-support system in which they might live, grow, and serve the Lord.

For those still seeking to be both disciples and disciple-makers, it is encouraging to know that the Eleven, led by the Holy Spirit, recorded (or supervised the writing down) for future generations all the major lessons that Jesus taught them. The result is that every essential Christian truth and the principles of Christian living have been preserved for disciples of all ages.

THE RELATIONSHIP OF JESUS TO DISCIPLEMAKERS AND NEW DISCIPLES

If Jesus instructs His disciples to go and make other disciples in the same manner in which He has trained them, a question rises about the relationship of the Eleven to other disciples whom they will raise up. Will they have exactly the same relationship to new disciples that Jesus has had with them? The matter is a problem for some who wonder how any disciplemaker today can assume the same role in relationship to those under his guidance that Jesus had in his relationship to His disciples. The charge is raised more bluntly by others who ask, "Does a disciplemaker try to play God in the lives of believers?" The fact that occasionally a spiritual leader has assumed too much authority over other disciples only accentuates the problem.

In response, consider two factors. First, the Eleven understand that the charge to make disciples has to do with making disciples of Jesus, not disciples of themselves. While people will become attached to them, and must do so in order that life-to-life transference can take place, their primary focus will be to make disciples of Jesus. One of their first responsibilities will be to assist new believers cultivate their relationship with the Lord. This accounts for their focus in Acts on encouraging younger Christians in the use of the means of grace. These "means" are designed so that newer believers might center their lives upon Jesus and cultivate their relationship to Him. Relationship to a disciplemaker or other spiritual leader is only another instrument to accomplish that objective.

JESUS AS DIVINE AND HUMAN

A second factor in a proper response to the accusation that disciplemakers are playing God includes a proper theological understanding of the person of Jesus. He is the divine, supernatural Son of God and at the same time fully human. The Incarnation binds God's supernatural person to created mankind. The result is that Jesus is absolutely unique, both God and man. This the church has always confessed in declaring Him to be "conceived by the Holy Spirit, born of the Virgin Mary." Jesus' dual nature means that He relates to His disciples in two ways. First, His divine nature means that He has an authority and power unique in the world. He teaches with authority because He speaks the Word of God. Further, it gives Him the power to work miracles as a demonstration that God is present among His people. Second, as the divine Son of God He represents God to them and for them because He *is* God.

Jesus not only relates to His disciples in His deity but in His humanity as well. He is the Son of God; He is also the Son of Man. Because He has taken on human nature, He has all the needs and emotions of a human being. He needs the fellowship of other people just as everyone does. It is primarily in His humanity that Jesus serves as a disciplemaker of the Twelve. The fact that He is incarnated in human flesh is the very thing that makes it possible for Him to invest His life over a period of three years in His men. Without the incarnation, life-to-life transference would be impossible. As a human being, then, Jesus is modeling certain lessons, instructing His disciples, holding them accountable, and pouring His life into them.

IMPLICATIONS OF JESUS' DUAL NATURE
FOR DISCIPLEMAKERS

An understanding of Jesus' dual nature clarifies the method of discipleship the Eleven will use. Jesus' disciples (and all future disciplemakers) can never relate to believers as a supernatural being can. They can never replace Jesus in other peoples' lives. In fact, their goal is to relate disciples directly to the person of Jesus. A disciplemaker's responsibility is to encourage believers to cultivate their relationship to Jesus, principally through prayer and study of the Word of God, so that they might develop a personal relationship with Him just as His first disciples did.

One implication of the fact that disciplemakers cannot replace Jesus in His deity is that disciples never carry the same authority over others that Jesus carried. The New Testament indicates that they do have a certain authority and responsibility as spiritual leaders of the people of God, but it is never absolute or unqualified authority like that of Jesus. The early church's recognition of this is demonstrated by the fact that most authority in the church at large and in local congregations is exercised by a group of men. Disciplemakers' authority must be qualified by the body of Christ. This is for the protection of the disciplemakers as well as the disciples. Take great care in this area so that proper biblical authority is not misused. Recognition of the fact that no spiritual leader's authority is ever absolute in the sense that Jesus' was should assist in proper understanding and balance of authority in the church.

While disciplemakers can never replace Jesus in His deity, in some sense, they must replace Him in His humanity. As disciplemakers, they are to do in the lives of others what Jesus did in their lives, i.e., invest themselves, train new disciples to grow in character and skill in using appropriate methods for serving God. Disciplemakers must also hold disciples accountable to enable them to get God's best. This means that the task of any disciplemaker will be slightly different from that of Jesus. Jesus does give His own disciples a pattern, however, by helping them cultivate their relationship with the Father. Now all future disciplemakers must help younger disciples cultivate their relationship with the Father, the Son, and the Spirit. At the same time, they must invest their lives in younger Christians.

Conversely, believers seeking to be trained as disciples of Jesus must also learn to cultivate two relationships. One is a direct relationship with Jesus; the second is a relationship with a disciplemaker. Since the disciplemaker primarily represents the humanity of Jesus, he or she carries a delegated authority to do His task and therefore carries some responsibility for new disciples. But any attempt to make a disciplemaker the final word in the life of any disciple in a contemporary setting is without proper foundation.

TIME AND MAKING DISCIPLES

The Eleven understand that there is a crucial time element involved in the process of obedience to Jesus' commission. They understand that Jesus is giving them a lifetime responsibility, not a short-term task. This is a permanent assignment that they are to carry out for the rest of their lives. Becoming a disciplemaker is not a temporary interlude. It is a way of life.

Second, they understand that a sizeable amount of time is essential to accomplish in other peoples' lives what Jesus has accomplished with and in them. He has invested in them full time for three years. To equal the number of hours in the lives of others will be an ongoing process over a period of years. This will be especially true when a full-time relationship is impossible.

So while the decision initially to believe on the Lord might come within a short period of time, the process of turning a believer into a disciple is understood to be a lengthy one. Any attempt to cut short this process will by its very nature undermine Jesus' purposes and instructions. Contemporary disciplemakers must not overlook the implications of this factor. Few contemporary discipleship relationships are full-time, living-in-community situations. To have the same amount of time for training requires a greater number of years than Jesus invested in His own disciples. The task is not a brief one. Failure to recognize this can easily lead to disillusionment and/or discouragement on the part of both the disciplemaker and the disciple.

THE PRINCIPLE OF CONCENTRATION

Jesus' command to make disciples includes the principle of concentration. Because, by its very nature, discipleship involves such a significant investment of time and energy in the life transference process, a disciplemaker can invest only in a few people. Thus while Jesus had a sizeable public ministry, a significant share of His ministry was focused upon only a few.

The principle of concentration may be illustrated in Jesus' life by a series of concentric circles. The outer circle represents unbelievers to whom Jesus had some ministry, primarily in outdoor preaching, healing, and casting out of demons. The next circle includes those who responded to Him by faith and who began in some initial way to follow Him—those who came regularly to hear Him preach or teach as well as a few personal friends with whom He associated. Certainly, some among the 120 in the Upper Room at Pentecost as well as a number among the 500 who saw Him after the Resurrection would be numbered in this group of those who became believers in Jesus. The third circle includes the Seventy who were closer to Jesus and were in training under Him for spiritual maturation and service for Him. The Seventy represented a transition group from the larger number of believers to the dozen in whom Jesus made His primary investment.

It is the circle of twelve, of course, that represents His primary focus of concentration. Among His personal relationships they receive the major share of His life-to-life investment. But even of the Twelve Jesus spends more time with three. On significant occasions in His life, as on the Mount of Transfiguration, the raising of Jairus' daughter, and His agony in Gethsemane, He particularly wants with Him Peter, James, and John. Finally, some think that of the three He may be closest to one, viz., John the Apostle. John seems to be the one whom Jesus loved in a special way. This would reflect Jesus' own need as a human being for a close relationship to a few on an even more intimate basis. Like others, He sought out a smaller circle from among those particularly close to Him, and even among that close circle He may have had a best friend. In His deity, of course, He loved them all equally, but in His humanity He was certainly closer to some than others. This is a part of God's divine plan for making disciples of all nations.

THE PRINCIPLE OF MULTIPLICATION

Another strategic principle related to making disciples is that of multiplication. Because Jesus concentrated upon a few, He could train them well enough for them to train a few others. Only with the principle of concentration can the quality of training be significant enough for others to learn how to make additional disciples. In other words, multiplication is possible only where there is serious concentration. The principle of multiplication in Jesus' strategy for touching the whole world has already been discussed, so it is sufficient to note here that this concept is solidly linked with the concept of concentrating on a few people in discipleship.

The reverse connection between these two principles, concentration and multiplication, is also true. Those who refuse to concentrate on a few people in a private discipleship kind of ministry will never multiply themselves to touch the world significantly for God. There is a limit on how far one individual can stretch his or her own gifts, time, and energy in public ministry. While much direct good may be accomplished in public ministry, it is a strategy that basically short-circuits Jesus' plan for reaching as many people as possible for His purposes. Further, Jesus is not only concerned about the number of people affected but about the quality of what happens by grace in their lives. All contemporary attempts to make disciples must take Jesus' plan seriously. They must consider both the quality of godly character and fruitful service in the lives of disciples and the number of people who are touched by God's grace.

AT THE CENTER
OF THE GREAT COMMISSION

Jesus commands His disciples to make disciples (Matt. 28:19–20). Remember that clustered around the main verb, "make disciples," are three participles that spell out something of the process that is implied by that imperative. The reference to "going" and making disciples of all nations signals that the disciples are to take the initiative in reaching other people. They are not to wait for people to come to them; they are to go where people are and can hear the gospel and respond to it. The going and teaching of all nations injects a geographical element in fulfillment of the Great Commission, and this gives it an international flavor (see also Acts 1:8).

Further, "going" demonstrates God's concern for all the peoples of the earth. He began to express that concern when He called Abraham to follow Him (Gen. 12:3) and when He chose Israel to be a people of His own possession because all the earth was His (Ex. 19:5–6). The making of disciples of all *nations* means of all *ethnos* or ethnic groups. It has to do with people groups in various nations, i.e., different linguistic, geographical, cultural, and sub-cultural groupings. The pattern for making disciples is graphically illustrated by Jesus' instructions in Acts 1:8, when He tells His disciples they will be witnesses to Him in Jerusalem, Judea and Samaria, and the uttermost parts of the earth. They are to begin making disciples at home in a process that will spread in an ever-widening circle eventually to touch the whole world.

While disciplemaking is international in scope, reference to the Great Commission is often used in contemporary circles only to refer to missionary activity in a foreign culture. Further, it usually focuses upon church planting, education, agriculture, medicine, and a host of other missionary ministries. A close look at the context of what Jesus said to His disciples reminds us that the central thrust of the Great Commission is the process of making disciples just as Jesus has made them. Certainly we must do this overseas, but no more than it needs to be done wherever one happens to reside. Those not making disciples at home are not likely to be effective at making disciples in another cultural setting. While many Christian ministries in the world are valuable, they cannot fulfill the heart of the Great Commission unless they include a private, concentrated ministry to a few people, aiding them to become disciplined followers of Jesus. Everyone committed to fulfilling the Great Commission must regularly ask, "Am I following Jesus' method to accomplish His purpose?"

THE FIRST PART OF THE GREAT COMMISSION: OUTREACH

Besides going where people are in order to reach them for Christ, the Great Commission includes two other elements in its description of disciplemaking. The first is in Jesus' command to "baptize them in the name of the Father, the Son, and of the Holy Spirit." In the New Testament, baptism is an outward sign to indicate a newly established commitment to Jesus Christ. In the Great Commission, baptism seems to represent the culmination of the whole process of outreach. This outreach, or evangelism, in turn, includes three factors: 1) proclamation of the gospel so that men and women might understand their sinfulness, God's offer of saving grace, and the need for their response to obtain salvation; 2) bringing people to a decision of faith in Christ and a commitment of their lives to Him, resulting in their justification by God and their new birth into His spiritual family; 3) public declaration of this new allegiance to Jesus Christ. In the early church this is done in baptism. The baptism element of the Great Commission, then, is not concerned only with baptizing people; it is a shorthand method of delineating the entire process of evangelism.

In addition, baptism in the name of the Father, the Son, and the Holy Spirit indicates that new believers now have a new relationship to all three members of the triune Godhead. They have entered the kingdom of God, begun to follow

Jesus, and been born of the Spirit. Not only do believers have a new relationship with God, they also have a new nature within. This is suggested by baptism in the name of God, that is, in the nature of God. This new nature is one of the results of the new birth that brings transforming grace into the lives of believers. The baptismal formula clearly points to the essential character of that nature through reference to the Spirit of God as the *Holy* Spirit. Through the experience of salvation by grace, God begins to make people holy as He is holy. The process of making disciples begins when men and women come into an experience of salvation where these two things happen, and when they witness publicly to them.

THE SECOND PART OF THE GREAT COMMISSION: TRAINING

Jesus points to the second aspect of making disciples when He adds, "teaching them to observe all that I have commanded you" (Matt. 28:20). If the first dimension of making disciples has to do with evangelism, the second has to do with training those who have made a decision to follow Jesus. In a sense this is where disciplemaking proper begins, when a disciplemaker starts to teach new believers what it means to be a disciplined follower of Jesus.

Jesus instructs the Eleven to teach others to observe all that He has commanded them. The word *observe* really means to obey, reminding all new disciples to place themselves under the authority of Jesus. The disciples are to teach new believers everything that Jesus commanded them. This implies more than formal commands, for it suggests knowledge of every principle and every exhortation that Jesus gave to His followers. Thus the Eleven were not to pass along only part of what Jesus had taught them but everything that had been built into their lives.

Many feel that once new believers decide to follow Christ the Great Commission has been fulfilled. For some parts of the church, completing the process of evangelism is sufficient. But from Jesus' perspective that does not finish the task of making disciples. Until people are trained as Jesus trained the Twelve, real discipleship will not have taken place. This is particularly significant for contemporary evangelicalism which places such a heavy stress on outreach, but gives only minimal time and energy even to initial follow-up. That step is the *beginning* of a discipleship process, but it is nothing like the extensive training Jesus envisioned when He spoke the Great Commission.

Perhaps it is not surprising, then, to find such a large number of "babes" in Christ, and so few godly men and women of real maturity in the faith. Frankly, it is much easier to proclaim the gospel, bring people to a decision of faith, and get a public commitment for Christ than it is to teach and train them to be disciplined followers of Jesus. The first part of fulfilling the Great Commission may be completed in a relatively short period of time. The second half of the Great Commission, by its very nature, requires extensive time and energy spent over a period of several years.

Jesus makes His instructions explicit to His own disciples for several reasons. First, He knows that if new believers are not trained they can spiritually die and be lost. We observe in Jesus' ministry that many start out to follow Him and then turn away (e.g., John 6:66). Yet Jesus is not concerned only about their falling away, but also about their spiritual growth. Since His ultimate goals include godliness of character and training for fruitful service, He is not content for individuals just to believe on Him so that they can go to heaven. He is interested in far more than helping them escape hell. He is looking for men and women who are 1) like Him, 2) living in fellowship with Him, and 3) doing His will in the world.

Such a life only begins at conversion. Development of all three areas is essential, and the discipleship process is God's means of accomplishing those ends. Any plan that stops short of fulfilling both halves of the Great Commission is inconsistent with Jesus' purposes. Any practice of ministry which omits either part of making disciples is biblically incomplete in its design. Far too often contemporary evangelicalism has contented itself with getting decisions for Christ rather than making disciples for Him.

Finally, the great promise of the consistent presence of Jesus is made specifically to those who are making disciples. "I am with you always, to the close of the age." Other places in the Scriptures indicate that every believer enjoys the continuous presence of the Lord. But this particular promise is specifically for those who enjoy an intimate relationship with Jesus and who are sent out to do His will in the world, especially in terms of making disciples. He who made them into disciples now promises His personal presence as they go to make other disciples. It comes as a great encouragement to disciplemakers to know that Jesus, under whose authority they live, has not left them alone in the work, but has promised His personal presence to accomplish the task of making disciples, multiplying godly men and women, and touching all nations for God.

8

spirit-filled disciples

PREPARATION FOR THE COMING
OF THE HOLY SPIRIT

Jesus spent the night before His death in close conversation with His disciples. John records those hours in significant detail (John 13–17) because they represent Jesus' last important teaching to His disciples. What He says is vividly impressed upon their minds and hearts. He is preparing them both for His departure and for the coming of the Holy Spirit into their lives in a new way on the day of Pentecost. The fact that Jesus says more about the relationship between the Holy Spirit and the disciples in these chapters from John's Gospel than in all His other teaching on the Holy Spirit indicates how important it was to Jesus that His disciples understand the Holy Spirit's role in their lives.

Although He is preparing them for the coming of Holy Spirit and His fuller work in their lives, Jesus indicates that the disciples are acquainted with the Holy Spirit already. He tells them that the non-Christian world cannot receive the Holy Spirit. But when He speaks about the relationship of the Spirit to His disciples, He says, "You know Him, for He dwells with you" (John 14:17). This corresponds to what Jesus has said elsewhere (John 3), that everyone who comes into the kingdom of God must be born of the Spirit. Jesus

reveals that the new birth takes place by the agency of the
Holy Spirit so that everyone experiencing the new birth also
begins a personal relationship with the Holy Spirit (John
3:3–8).

What Jesus says to the Eleven is true of every subsequent
follower of the Lord. Everyone who believes in the Lord
Jesus Christ and is born into the family of God receives the
Holy Spirit initially. All Christians begin to know the Holy
Spirit, and He dwells with them as the personal presence of
God in their lives. Any discussion about the coming of the
fullness of God's Spirit in disciples' lives must be prefaced
with an understanding that all Christians already have the
Holy Spirit within. A personal relationship with the third
member of the Trinity, which begins at conversion, is as real
as the relationships with the Father and the Son. The fact that
Jesus took so much time the last evening with His disciples to
talk about the Holy Spirit indicates that He is vitally
concerned that every disciple both understand the work of the
Spirit and experience His fullness just as the Twelve did.

THE PROMISE OF THE HOLY SPIRIT

After Jesus' death and Resurrection He meets with His
disciples on several occasions for brief instructions. The next
to the last of His commandments during this time is the
giving of the Great Commission, which we have already
examined in some detail. Luke records, however, that in His
final instructions Jesus tells them that He will send to them
"the promise of the Father." This is coupled with the
command that they remain in Jerusalem until they are
"clothed with power from on high" (Luke 24:49). It is this
waiting in Jerusalem for the promise of the Father that will be
rewarded, said Jesus, when "before many days you shall be
baptized with the Holy Spirit" (Acts 1:4–5).

While the command to wait to be baptized with the Holy
Spirit is Jesus' ultimate instruction to His disciples, it should
not have surprised the disciples nor any subsequent readers of
the Gospels. In the introductions to the person of Jesus in all

four Gospels, John the Baptist declares that Jesus would baptize with the Holy Spirit (Matt. 3:11; Mark 1:8; Luke 3:16; John 1:33). Thus the public ministry of Jesus is introduced four times with a promise that Jesus will send the Holy Spirit to His disciples in this way. Now at the end of His last post-resurrection appearance with them, He commands them to wait for this experience. In a sense, the references to the baptism of the Holy Spirit for disciples bracket the whole gospel story and therefore need to be given careful attention.

THE NECESSITY OF THE FULLNESS OF THE HOLY SPIRIT

Biblical data indicate that Jesus feels that His disciples are not ready to begin their public and private ministry on their own without the fullness of God's Holy Spirit. This principle that no disciple is ready to make other disciples without the fullness of God's Spirit is illustrated in Jesus' own life. He Himself does not embark upon His own ministry until the descent of the Holy Spirit upon Him during His baptism (Matt. 3:16; Mark 1:10; Luke 3:22; John 1:32). Because of His sinless nature, Jesus did not need baptism for the forgiveness of sins, nor did He require the fullness of the Spirit for cleansing from a sinful nature. But he experienced them as part of His symbolic identification with fallen mankind, which needs both.

In His humanity Jesus models for His disciples the need for the power of the Holy Spirit to do God's work and ministry effectively in the world. Consequently, while the descent of the Holy Spirit upon Jesus as He begins His own ministry may be somewhat different from the coming of the Holy Spirit to the disciples at Pentecost, there are clearly some parallels. Jesus demonstrates before the disciples that they are not ready to minister for God without His full control over their lives through an experience of the baptism of the Holy Spirit. If Jesus is the great disciplemaker, then the example He sets before others is indispensable for future disciples. His pattern implies that no disciple is fully ready for public ministry or the private concentrated ministry of making disciples without an experience of the infilling of the Holy Spirit.

THE ROLE OF PENTECOST IN THE LIVES OF DISCIPLES

Some have argued that since the events of Pentecost are historical phenomena, and thus in a sense not repeatable, subsequent disciples need not feel compelled to seek a similar experience in their own lives. Unquestionably, the day of Pentecost was a distinct historical event and in the sense that it represents the birth of the New Testament church, its events are indeed unique and not repeatable. Yet may it not simultaneously present a deeper sanctifying work of God's Spirit in the lives of disciples, and in that sense represent a necessary event in the life of every disciple of Jesus? Certainly many other things the disciples experienced had a unique historical context. When Jesus first called them to follow Him (Matt. 4:18–22), that experience in its time, setting, circumstances, and manner was a unique historical event, and in that sense it was not to be repeated. But it was a historical experience illustrating the principle that Jesus wants to call all believers to be disciples. The call to follow Him and be made into fishers of men is an experience He extends to every believer in every age. In a similar manner, the infilling of the Holy Spirit in the lives of the disciples becomes a model of what Jesus desires in the life of everyone in any age who seeks to be a disciple and a disciplemaker.

THE PURPOSE OF THE INFILLING OF THE HOLY SPIRIT

For two reasons Jesus commands His disciples to wait for the fullness of the Spirit. First, He knows that even after three years of the discipleship process, God must still do something in the lives of the disciples in terms of their character.

Development and growth in their likeness to God has occurred, but something more needs to be done, particularly in regard to their self-centeredness. He knows that they need a purifying experience so that their wills and lives are at one with God. They are not fully ready to be a holy people representing a holy God until the Holy Spirit has taken entire control of them so that their character is reflective of the character of God.

Jesus also knows that for the disciples to serve God in ministry, and in particular to make other disciples, they cannot effectively work without both God's total control and His power flowing through their lives. They need the empowering Spirit of God if they are to do His will effectively in the world. While in training under His direction, they have been involved in certain types of ministry. Yet He knows that without His physical presence the disciples need God's empowerment to do effectively all that God designs for them. And this, He also knows, will come only with the fullness of the Spirit.

The needs that the Eleven demonstrate also appear in subsequent disciples of Jesus. This suggests that all those who would be like Him and serve Him fully need the experience of the infilling of the Holy Spirit. Because effective discipleship is dependent upon the infilling of the Holy Spirit, we must examine the relationship of these experiences to each other if contemporary disciples are fully to experience both. Jesus is not satisfied with having either the discipleship process or the fullness of the Holy Spirit, but He desires both for those who belong to Him.

THE SIGNIFICANCE OF THE INFILLING OF THE HOLY SPIRIT FOR DISCIPLESHIP

The role of the infilling/baptism of the Holy Spirit for discipleship is significant in three major areas. Not surprisingly, the first is the area of character: what the disciples are to be. A second area relates to what they are to do, the work to which Jesus has called them. The third area links the first two: what the disciples are to be and what they are to do.

THE MAKING OF GODLY CHARACTER

Even after Pentecost God is still looking for holy people. In other words, He continues to seek people of godly character. Believers cannot be a holy people without coming to be like the Father or like the Son, and the experience of the fullness of the Spirit is a part of that process. The Spirit makes His impact felt in at least four ways.

Character and the Full Control of the Holy Spirit

The first of these ways is that this fullness of the Spirit places the will of the disciple under the full control of the Holy Spirit. God thus can work out His holy character in a disciple's life in a much more complete way than before. God's character is communicated through His will, then from His will to the disciple's will, and lastly through the disciple's will to the disciple's character. If the will of the individual is wholly submitted to the will of God, then His holy character can be translated into the character of a disciple.

This transformation is described in a number of different ways, since it is so complex that no one figure of speech adequately describes all that occurs in this event. When a disciple's will, which controls his character, is completely submitted to the control of the will of God, which is directed by His holy character, this experience of submission may be described in terms of the baptism or infilling of the Holy Spirit. But it also may be seen as the cleansing or purification of the sinful nature, or self-will (2 Cor. 7:1). At other times it may be called entire sanctification (1 Thess. 5:23), or described in terms of a heart made perfect in love (Matt. 5:43–48). Each of these terms refers to a different dimension of that commitment.

When the will of the disciple is surrendered to God's will, it is completely controlled by the will of God through His Holy Spirit. The "entireness" of sanctification refers in part to the entire consecration of the will, and therefore the life, to a holy God. The fullness of the Spirit may further be defined as a purifying from sinfulness or self-will. After such an experience, one can no longer be even partially controlled by self-will, if one's will has been submitted completely to the will of God. Further, at that moment the individual's motives are changed, and he or she is given a motivation in the heart to love as God loves, i.e., unconditionally. This is usually described in terms of perfect love.

All of the above takes place at that point of crisis called the infilling of the Spirit, which centers on a disciple's will being completely under the control of God's will. Yet this momentous experience of consecration must be understood in the continuing translation from will to character. Two dimensions in particular are of special significance for translating the experience of the surrender of the will into godly character.

First, the disciple is often described as manifesting "perfect love." This deals primarily with a basic attitude toward other people. The other area in which a consecrated will is worked out through character is in terms of righteous living. This is the question of total obedience in a disciple's conduct. While the surrender of the will to the fullness of God's Spirit takes place in a moment, the working out of its implications in godly character, particularly in attitudes and conduct, is the process of growth after the infilling of the Holy Spirit. Here discipleship becomes absolutely essential for sanctified living. In these areas of learning to apply a heart of perfect love and a life of ethical righteousness in all behavior, a disciple urgently needs the spiritual disciplines of discipleship and the model of a disciplemaker.

The Holy Spirit and a Teachable Spirit

Second, the infilling of the Spirit affects character by making the disciple willing to grow. A disciple purged of self-will and the sinful nature by the baptism of the Spirit will be more teachable. The Holy Spirit, now in more nearly complete control, will be able to work out the holy character of God in the disciple's character, particularly in the areas of attitudes and conduct. The implications of godliness no longer threaten the self-orientation. Therefore, with a more teachable spirit, the disciple can now experience real growth and maturity.

The Holy Spirit and Discipline

Third, the infilling of the Holy Spirit affects the character by providing power for a more disciplined life. One cleansed from self-will has dealt with the most significant problem of discipline, i.e., the denial of self. Discipline always means denying oneself in order to accomplish more significant goals. Having recognized the need for dealing with his independent self-will, the disciple can now receive help from the Holy Spirit to make spiritual disciplines more effective in his or her life.

The Holy Spirit and Victorious Living

Fourth, the infilling of the Holy Spirit has such an impact on the life of a disciple because with this experience comes power for victorious Christian living. Once self-will has been overcome, the ability to resist temptation, which appeals chiefly to the self, is much greater. Then consistent victory over sin becomes possible.

LIVING UNDER GOD'S FULL AUTHORITY

Linking character and ministry is the disciple's response to authority. Here again the fullness of the Holy Spirit is essential. Authority and holiness meet in the conditions for receiving the baptism of the Spirit. These conditions are the same as those of a disciple who is living under the absolute authority of God as King. Two things are necessary in both: first, total consecration of the life to God, that is, a surrender of self-will and complete willingness to obey. Second, total trust or faith that makes possible total consecration. Full consecration and complete faith in God are also the conditional elements for the infilling of the Spirit, and thus are crucially bound up in what the grace of God does in changing a disciple's character to make it holy. But consecration and trust also are intimately wrapped up in living under the authority of God as the absolute King over a disciple's life. This means that they are crucially bound up in what He directs a disciple to do with his or her life and ministry.

SERVING WITH THE POWER OF THE SPIRIT

Finally, the infilling of the Spirit makes its impact on the life of discipleship in the ministry to which disciples are called. This includes at least three things.

Witness

First, the fullness of the Spirit provides the power to be witnesses in Jerusalem, in Judea and Samaria, and to the most distant parts of the earth (Acts 1:8). This is the power for outreach, to be fishers of men, to be a kingdom of priests; it involves the power of the disciple to present the gospel to other people.

Disciplemaking

Second, the fullness of the Spirit directly relates to disciplemaking; individuals reproduce what they are. To make godly disciples, disciplemakers must be godly. Since Jesus calls all disciples to contribute to the fulfillment of the Great Commission, they must have the kind of character through the fullness of the Holy Spirit that will make it possible to produce other men and women whose character will be like that of Jesus. For purposes of disciplemaking by example, by association, and by teaching through life-to-life investment, the experience of the fullness of the Holy Spirit is essential.

Use of God's Gifts

Third, when the Holy Spirit comes in His fullness, He assumes control over the disciple's spiritual gifts, other God-given abilities, time, resources, and energy for the work of ministry. When the Spirit has this kind of complete responsibility in these areas, He may employ all of them to serve the body of Christ. The disciple finds it easier to discover a proper function in the body of Christ, since with the surrender of self-will, he or she is now available to be used of God according to His design in the church. Thus a disciple's gifts, abilities, time, and energy may all be directed for the accomplishment of God's full will for the body of Christ.

THE SIGNIFICANCE OF DISCIPLESHIP FOR SPIRIT-FILLED LIVING

Discipleship Essential to Maintain Fullness of the Spirit

The effects of discipleship upon the individual who has experienced the baptism of the Holy Spirit are primarily twofold. First, the disciple is enabled to maintain the experience of the infilling of the Holy Spirit. There is no unconditional security for the Spirit-filled life any more than there is for the experience of justification. Failure to recognize this has led some to assume (perhaps subconsciously) that the fullness of the Spirit is automatically permanent. Experience warns that this can be a deadly trap indeed. Not only can the experience be lost, it certainly will be unless the conditions of total consecration and total trust are continually met.

Within the discipleship context, we have not only the model and teaching of Jesus for assistance, but also the spiritual disciplines built into our lives. These are necessary for keeping us under the full control of God's sanctifying Spirit. These disciplines (e.g., daily time in the Scripture and private prayer), which were developed to help the disciple know and obey God, are now used in a fuller way. After being filled with the Spirit, a disciple is committed to know and trust God more completely and to walk by faith in full obedience to His perfect will. But how can one live under God's perfect will if one does not know that will? The answer is that without intake from God's Word, one cannot know

God's will. Thus the daily discipline of Bible study becomes one of the underpinnings of a life fully under God's control.

Another aspect of discipleship that assists in maintaining the experience of the fullness of the Spirit is regular fellowship with others committed to holy living. Consistent fellowship with a few other disciples provides a place for supportive accountability in one's spiritual life. Regular attention, then, will be given to spiritual examination. Accountability to others means continual self-examination by disciples to see whether they are walking in obedience to God's perfect will. In addition, fellowship with God's people may be one of His means of guidance for the individual. The life of discipleship then enables one to keep one's will and life under the full control of the Holy Spirit and thus maintain the experience of God's sanctifying grace.

Discipleship Essential for Further Growth

Second, discipleship makes possible spiritual growth after the infilling of the Holy Spirit, the working out of the implications of a life completely under His control. When the self-will of the sin nature has been dealt with, real growth can take place in the disciple. No longer is there the struggle between self-will and God's will. Now the spiritual disciplines learned in the discipleship process for the purpose of growth in godliness become even more significant. Following the experience of the infilling of the Holy Spirit these tools for knowing God's will can be applied without the struggle over whether to do that will. The sanctified individual urgently needs the spiritual disciplines to discover the full meaning of a heart of perfect love and of a life committed to ethical righteousness. For the full implications of God's total control of the will become apparent only through the study of the Word, significant time in prayer, regular meeting with a few other like-minded disciples, fasting to know God's will, and following the model of a disciplemaker.

Discipleship, then, is a critical element in Spirit-filled living. Discipleship makes it possible to maintain an experience of the baptism of the Holy Spirit and simultaneously to work out its full consequences in the attitudes, behavior, and interpersonal relationships of the individual. Failure to give proper attention to making disciples as a complement to preaching the fullness of the Spirit may explain why so many do not retain their experience of sanctifying grace; while others never seem to be able to make real spiritual progress after consecrating their lives to God's sanctifying Spirit.

9

first fulfillment
of the great commission

PREPARATION FOR DISCIPLEMAKING:
FULLNESS OF THE HOLY SPIRIT

The two final sets of instructions Jesus gives to His disciples are 1) to go make disciples and 2) to wait for the fullness of the Holy Spirit. The disciples understand clearly the significance of both commands as well as the order of priority. They recognize that they are not to start on their life vocation of making disciples until they have received "the promise of the Father" (Luke 24:49), and so they wait in Jerusalem for the baptism of the Holy Spirit (Acts 1:4–5).

The first part of Acts 2 tells of the coming of the Holy Spirit in His fullness (Acts 2:1–13). With the Spirit's coming in sanctifying power (Acts 2:4), the disciples' obedience to Jesus' last command is complete and the fulfillment of His promise has come to fruition. Thus when Peter stands on the day of Pentecost to address the multitude, He now is free to begin to fulfill the next-to-the-last of Jesus' commandments, viz., "make disciples." Significantly, when the Spirit comes in His fullness, the disciples are now ready to do what Jesus has trained and instructed them to do. Making disciples is now their first priority in their ministry for Him.

After the coming of the Holy Spirit in Acts 2, the disciples begin the first fulfillment of the Great Commission.

Both parts of the order are illustrated in the story of what happened on the day of Pentecost and immediately thereafter. While the second part of the assignment takes place over a longer period of time, the initial components that make it up are all present in this chapter.

FIRST HALF OF THE GREAT COMMISSION: EVANGELISM

Proclamation

The first half of the Great Commission begins with Peter's address on the day of Pentecost (Acts 2:14). It ends with the baptism of the three thousand (Acts 2:41). This outreach is centered in the proclamation of the gospel as Peter speaks for the rest. His pattern of preaching is instructive. He begins by basing his message on the Word of God (Acts 2:16–21), citing passages from the prophet Joel for two purposes. First, he uses the Word of God to explain the phenomenon of the giving of the fullness of God's Spirit in the Upper Room (Acts 2:17, 20; Joel 2:28–32). Second, he can then preach to them about Jesus as the Christ by taking as his text, "It shall be that whoever calls on the name of the Lord shall be saved" (Acts 2:21).

Having shifted the focus from the work of the Spirit in believers to the person of Jesus upon whom people must call for salvation, Peter proclaims and explains the gospel. First, he reminds them of Jesus' life and of the mighty works, wonders, and signs God did through Him in their midst (Acts 2:22). He then discusses God's purpose in Jesus' death. By the hands of lawless men, he explains, the Lord was crucified for the sins of the world (Acts 2:23). Next he dwells upon the Resurrection of Jesus as a sign that God has the power to give life over death. He implies that the God who gives physical life in the Resurrection is the same God who can give spiritual life to everyone believing in Him (see also Rom. 8:11).

Further, discussion of the Resurrection gives Peter opportunity to make the point that, since Jesus is still alive, one may relate to Him personally. The Apostle proclaims the exaltation of Jesus to the right hand of God and the pouring out of the Holy Spirit as a promise from God upon those who belong to Him (Acts 2:33–35). Finally, he argues that Jesus' Crucifixion, Resurrection, and Ascension demonstrate that God has declared Him to be both Lord and Christ. God has made clear that Jesus is the Lord of the universe and the Messiah for whom the Jews have been looking (Acts 2:36).

This example of the proclamation of the gospel demonstrates that to respond to the gospel of Jesus Christ people need certain basic information about who He is and what He came to do. All evangelism, whether by preaching, personal conversation, or writing, must include elements that help people understand the life, death, Resurrection, and Ascension of Jesus and His designated roles as Lord and Christ. Further, Peter has modeled for all future evangelism that the communication of the gospel must be firmly grounded in the Word of God. Not only does he begin there, but throughout his presentation he liberally cites other passages from Scripture. The use of the Word of God in this way adds a power in communication far above the natural capacities of anyone involved in outreach and evangelism.

Repentance and Faith

The process of evangelism is incomplete, however, with the proclamation of the gospel. Peter's preaching of God's Word leads to a decision of faith among His hearers. They are first "cut to the heart"; then they asked Peter what they should do (Acts 2:37). The proclamation of the gospel produced conviction in their hearts. They are able to see that what God has said through Peter is true, that they are under condemnation themselves and need to respond to God. Peter deals with their conviction of sin by explaining the need for repentance and the forgiveness of their sins (Acts 2:38). He knows how to respond to his hearers because he has listened to Jesus challenge people since the beginning of His ministry (Matt. 4:17; Mark 1:14–15). Because Peter has been discipled in Jesus' method of evangelism, he knows how to help people respond to God. Further, Peter's call to repentance and forgiveness implies that people will turn away from sin and ask for forgiveness because they believe God will forgive them. Thus, while Peter does not refer directly to faith, he clearly implies it. The choice on the part of hearers to believe in the Lord Jesus is spelled out elsewhere in responses to the gospel in the book of Acts (e.g., Acts 4:4).

The meaning of Peter's statement that his hearers "shall receive the gift of the Holy Spirit" (Acts 2:38), is not immediately clear. He may be referring to the initial gift of the Holy Spirit who comes into the life of every believer when he or she is born of the Spirit of God (John 3:5–6, 8). On the other hand, he may be pointing to the fullness of the Holy Spirit, like that which the apostles received in the Upper Room. If the latter is the case, Peter does not necessarily imply that the fullness of the Spirit will be an immediate fruit of their repentance, forgiveness, and faith in the Lord Jesus. Since Scripture does not refer to his hearers receiving the fullness of the Holy Spirit on that occasion, he clearly does not mean that the fullness of the Holy Spirit is an experience synonymous with conversion.

Public Commitment Through Baptism

After a further word of exhortation, those who receive the Word of God through Peter respond to his invitation. The results are that three thousand people make a decision of faith and seal it with a public witness to Jesus by means of baptism (Acts 2:41). Consequently, with the baptism of the 3,000 there comes the first fulfillment of the first half of the Great Commission. The process of evangelism has been completed, including the elements of proclamation, a decision of repentance and faith, and a public witness to a new relationship with the Lord. The first essential part of making disciples has been completed. No one can become a disciple of Jesus without going through this process.

SECOND HALF OF THE GREAT COMMISSION: TRAINING

The disciples understand that in order to make disciples they must bring people to the experience of baptism and, further, that they are to teach new believers all the things Jesus has taught them. Accordingly, right after the public declaration of the 3,000 regarding their commitment to Christ, the fulfillment of the second half of the Great Commission begins (Acts 2:42–47). This description in Acts, of course, is introductory. The training dimension of discipleship must occur over a period of years. Yet the essential elements of discipleship appear in these brief verses.

Luke records that the 3,000 new believers begin to commit themselves to certain spiritual disciplines. "They devoted themselves to the apostles' teaching and fellowship, to the breaking of bread and the prayers" (Acts 2:42). The word for "devote" is a strong one, implying deep commitment with an ongoing persistence. In other words, from the beginning they took seriously these crucial disciplines for spiritual growth.

Training in Doctrine

The new believers devoted themselves first to "the apostles' teaching" (Acts 2:42). A brief survey of subsequent chapters in Acts indicates that the content of the apostles' teaching includes the Old Testament, the teachings of Jesus, the life of Jesus, and the inspired interpretation of the gospel and its implications by the apostles themselves. These last three elements of the apostles' teaching form the heart of what has come down to us as the New Testament. The new Christians, then, are committing themselves to the Word of God as a basis for becoming disciples of Jesus. This was Jesus' plan when He instructed His disciples to teach them everything he had commanded them (Matt. 28:20). As a result, the new believers immediately got into the Word of God through the teaching of the apostles. Like previous generations of the people of God, they placed themselves under the authority of

God and His spoken word. From early on, the question of God's authority in their lives was a settled issue. For them, God's Word was the basis of all discipleship and spiritual growth. True doctrine based on the Word of God is essential both for growth to spiritual maturity and for being a disciple of Jesus.

Training in Prayer

These new Christians also learned quickly to devote themselves to the spiritual discipline of prayer. Reference to prayers (Acts 2:42) may include public prayers in the temple, prayer in small groups, and private prayers of individuals and families. Again, subsequent chapters in Acts indicate the many ways in which early Christians exercised this means of grace. But the crucial element is that they began to learn how to pray.

These two disciplines, living with God's Word and learning to pray, form the basis for the new believers' relationship to God. These are the primary tools for communicating with God. They must hear His voice through the Word of God, and they must speak with Him by means of prayer. This explains why commitment to a daily personal devotional time, both in the Word of God and in prayer, is indispensable for a disciple of Jesus.

Training in Worship

A third discipline to which the disciples devoted themselves was "the breaking of bread" (Acts 2:42). Some feel this may be a sub-category of fellowship, that this may refer to the agape meal in the early church. Others think it is an indirect reference to the breaking of bread in Holy Communion. If the latter is true, this practice would therefore have more direct relevance to public worship. The early church was committed to both. If "breaking of bread" means taking Communion, it shows how important public worship was for the early Christians. What the disciples learned from Jesus about attending the synagogue as a regular custom is now passed on to others who are becoming disciples.

Training in Fellowship

A fourth discipline to which the new believers devote themselves is fellowship (Acts 2:42). This includes fellowship with the apostles themselves, but also fellowship with one another. Although "fellowship" today often means only very casual relationships, in the early church it involved a much greater intimacy centered in spiritual things. This is suggested by Acts 2:42 in which this kind of fellowship is bracketed by the Word of God and prayer. Fellowship here is based upon a common commitment, both to believe in Jesus and to follow after Him as His disciples. This fellowship produces a type of bonding about which non-Christians know very little.

Christians' fellowship may be subdivided into two sorts. Luke indicates that day by day they were "attending the temple together and breaking bread in their homes" (Acts 2:46). Attending the temple together certainly means fellowship with a large group of other Christians. This fellowship of the congregation demonstrates the early church's commitment to public worship, the occasion for teaching, preaching, and praise. It reminds all disciples of the necessity of regularly meeting with the larger body of Christ. Meeting together serves as a consistent reminder that no believer is alone. Spiritual blessing and psychological encouragement follow from membership in a large fellowship of people who are seeking God.

The second form of fellowship described was their practice of meeting in their homes (Acts 2:46). The church was broken down into small groups that met throughout the city, the size of the group determined by the amount of living space in a Palestinian home, probably somewhere between six and twelve. Consequently, the early church not only met in large groups for fellowship, but also in small groups as a part of their training and edification. This is consistent with the understanding the Eleven had regarding their own training as disciples. Jesus had taught them in a small group, and if others were to become disciples they must also relate intimately to a few other believers with similar purpose and commitment. Apparently this process of regular meeting with a small group began early in the life of the church.

Training in Giving

The other spiritual discipline alluded to in Acts 2 is that of giving. Because of God's work of grace in their hearts, the new believers began to share their possessions. Where needs existed in the congregation, they were met by distribution of resources to all as needs arose. Early on they received Jesus' teaching about giving, about seeking first God's kingdom and His righteousness, and about trusting God to provide all things necessary for their physical existence (Matt. 6:2–4, 33). While the form of giving changes throughout Acts, e.g., the holding of all things in common, the principle of giving continues to be illustrated in the lives of all those serious about being disciples of Jesus (Acts 4:32–37; 11:29–30).

The Results of Training

It is evident that out of the disciples' own commitment to key spiritual disciplines they began to build these habits into the lives of new Christians. The essential disciplines described include commitment to the Word of God, to prayer, to fellowship, to public worship, and to giving. If Peter's preaching on the day of Pentecost illustrates the significance of Scripture memory (Acts 2:17–21, 25–28, 34–35), then all of the major spiritual disciplines that Jesus first set out for His disciples were demonstrated in the early church, with the exception of fasting which appears later (cf. Acts 13:2).

It may well be that out of the training received in discipleship, the new believers also began to learn how to share the gospel. Certainly it is out of the overflow of their lives that many others were attracted to the gospel and drawn into the fellowship of God's people. Because the disciples began immediately with both halves of the Great Commission, the result was continued growth of the church. "The Lord added to their number day by day those who were being saved" (Acts 2:47).

The depth of the new believers' commitment and their training to be disciplined followers of Jesus results in an ongoing multiplication process. God does not continue to use only apostles to proclaim the gospel and draw men and women to Himself. Now He works through the entire group of those being formed into disciples. Thus the place of spiritual disciplines revealed that God's grace was at work in the new Christians: first, in their character (illustrated by their concern for one another in giving); and, second, in service to the Body of Christ and the world (illustrated by the large number of people coming into the church through their witness).

The pattern of training in the early church, then, was parallel to that of Jesus. They are concerned with the same objectives of producing godly men and women whom the Lord could use in fruitful service for His kingdom. The means of accomplishing this include both an experience of God's redeeming grace and discipleship training that results in spiritual maturity. Discipleship training in particular includes a commitment to certain spiritual habits that enhance their relationship with God and a commitment to their service for Him, other believers, and the world. Because Jesus did His job well in training disciples, the Eleven were able to do the same for others. These lessons must not be lost upon the church today. We must first recover the basic principles underlying our role as disciples of Jesus. Then we must begin effectively to help others implement the same principles in their lives through the process of making disciples.

10

ỏISCIPLEMAKING IN THE EARLY CHURCH

Jesus gave His disciples instructions to go and make disciples. Immediately after the coming of the Holy Spirit on the day of Pentecost they began that work. In Acts 2 we get a glimpse of the first steps they took. How well did they follow through with the Lord's design? Were they really trained well enough to reproduce themselves in others? What did those new Christians look like at the end of the process? Further, when they in turn discipled others, what kind of followers of Jesus did they turn out to be? One way to evalulate their effectiveness is to take a close look at members of the early church who were one or two generations removed from the apostles.

BARNABAS

One of the people in the early church whose life answers these questions is Barnabas. He is a little-known but influential figure. His story illustrates the kind of disciple and disciplemaker produced by the apostles. Barnabas also provides us a glimpse of the disciplemaking process as employed by someone other than Jesus. In addition, this example should strengthen our resolve to be involved in the disciplemaking process ourselves. If someone other than Jesus can actually make disciples, then by His grace perhaps we can do it as well.

Barnabas first appears in Acts 4. Peter and John were called before the Sanhedrin where they bore testimony to Jesus before the Jewish leaders, doing so with a holy boldness that came from the power of God's Spirit. After their release, they returned to tell the other believers about what the Lord had done. At that point the new Christians realized that they did not have this same power for witness. They began to pray about the matter, and the record says that they were "all filled with the Holy Spirit" and spoke "the word of God with boldness" (Acts 4:31). As an outflow of this new spiritual power, those who believed began to hold things in common and share their possessions for the care of the needy. The person whom Luke chose as an example of this caring ministry was Barnabas. "Joseph who was surnamed by the apostles Barnabas (which means, son of encouragement), a Levite, a native of Cyprus, sold a field which belonged to him, and brought the money and laid it at the apostles' feet" (Acts 4:36–37).

His name was really Joseph, but as he became a part of the community of faith and the apostles got better acquainted with him, they identified his spiritual gift. This gift orientation, that of exhortation or encouragement, resulted in a new name. This often happens in Scripture as an indicator of God's power to transform lives. So they named him Barnabas, "son of encouragement" or "son of exhortation." It is important to note that the apostles were able to do this only because of a close day-by-day relationship between Barnabas and themselves.

Barnabas was a Levite, a Jew. But as a native of Cyprus, he had grown up in the gentile world rather than in Palestine. He was a part of the Diaspora, the Jews who were spread abroad throughout the eastern end of the Mediterranean. Because he was both Jewish and from outside Palestine, Barnabas was doubly qualified for service. His Jewish background gave him a heritage from among the people of God and a familiarity with the Old Testament as well as knowledge of Jewish customs. Yet because he had grown up in the

Greek-speaking world, he knew pagan customs, culture, patterns of thought, interests, spiritual hungers, and ways they might be reached with the gospel. God in His sovereignty used this rich background to prepare Barnabas to bridge the worlds of Jewish Christianity and the Gentiles.

Apparently Barnabas was a man of some means, for he owned a field near Jerusalem. He sold the property and brought the money to the apostles to help meet the needs of some among the believers. God had touched him. Because of this he gave out of a growing spiritual sensitivity to others' needs. Evident in Barnabas is the discipline of giving.

BARNABAS INTRODUCES PAUL
TO THE CHURCH

Barnabas does not appear again in the narrative of the early church until Acts 9. This chapter tells of Paul's conversion. In it is recorded that dramatic Damascus road experience of Paul's confrontation with the Lord he had been persecuting. Immediately after his conversion Paul began to minister in Damascus. Somewhat later, when forced to escape from that city, he returned to Jerusalem. Luke described his reception: "When he had come to Jerusalem he attempted to join the disciples; and they were all afraid of him, for they did not believe that he was a disciple" (Acts 9:26). Leaders of the early church were astute men. They knew Paul as a crafty character and they could easily imagine what he might be up to. They probably thought to themselves, "It's just like Paul to pretend to be a believer in the Way, come in and find out where we all meet, who the leaders are, where we live, what times we gather, then return later to round us up and haul us off to prison. We are not about to touch him." Their fears were justified, for this is just the kind of thing Paul might have done. He was like that.

"But Barnabas took him," Luke reports, "and brought him to the apostles, and declared to them how on the road he had seen the Lord, who spoke to him, and how at Damascus he had preached boldly in the name of Jesus" (Acts 9:27).

Barnabas was the key to getting Paul into the church. Important in itself, the action also reveals something significant about this "son of encouragement."

First, it indicates his tremendous courage. Interviewing the former chief enemy of the church is like putting your head in a lion's mouth. If Paul had turned out not to be a Christian, Barnabas would certainly have been imprisoned whether or not anyone else was. Second, the episode shows his sensitivity to the Spirit of God beyond any courage native to himself. The Holy Spirit led him, and he was aware of that.

Third, some discernment on Barnabas' part is necessary to see into Paul's heart, to listen to his testimony of how the Lord had appeared to him, and then to hear how God had begun to work through his life as he ministered in Damascus. Barnabas judged that Paul's conversion was genuine. Grace had touched Paul, and he stood before him now as a new creature in Christ, a genuine believer desiring to join with other followers of the Lord. Fourth, this event indicates a close relationship between Barnabas and the apostles. It is so close that the apostles were willing for Barnabas to bring their former chief enemy into their midst. Clearly they had great confidence in Barnabas' spiritual discernment and judgment. This knowledge of Barnabas and his abilities could result only from a close relationship between himself and some of the apostles.

What is not clear is the question of which apostle discipled Barnabas. Hints in Scripture may point to Peter, but the data are not strong enough for a firm conclusion. Obviously, though, someone invested in Barnabas and knew him well enough to trust his judgment. As a result, Barnabas was able to get Paul into the church by affirming the genuineness of Paul's conversion experience. Paul then moved in and out among them until the church sent him away to Tarsus for his own protection (Acts 9:30).

BARNABAS SENT TO ANTIOCH

We do not see Barnabas again until Acts 11. The context tells of the believers who were scattered abroad because of the persecution of Stephen. Many fled to Phoenicia, Cyprus, and Antioch where they spread the Word to "none except Jews." But some of them, men of Cyprus and Cyrene, came to Antioch and spoke to the Greeks also, preaching the Lord Jesus. The result was that "the hand of the Lord was with them, and a great number that believed turned to the Lord" (Acts 11:20–21). The first half of the Great Commission was thus carried out in Antioch.

When this news reached the church in Jerusalem, leaders realized that Jesus' commandment was not only to get converts in places like Antioch, but *to make disciples*. Accordingly, they wanted to send an experienced disciplemaker to do so. Barnabas was ready for this assignment. Not only was he ready, but because of his background among Gentiles he was uniquely fitted for this ministry. Antioch was a gentile city with a Greek-speaking Christian community.

Barnabas' fitness for this responsibility is demonstrated by the fact that he is the only person in the book of Acts whom the church leadership sends out alone. Perhaps this says something about their confidence in him. It probably also indicates that they know some of the people already in Antioch who are busy preaching and teaching the Word, and they are aware that he would not be alone there. Further, they are confident that he is well trained in team ministry so that he will not remain by himself very long. As a result of their trust in him, they send him to begin to fulfill the second half of the Great Commission—that of discipling the new believers there.

When Barnabas arrived in Antioch "and saw the grace of God, he was glad." He recognized a genuine work of God's grace by which people were being changed rather than a spurious movement characterized by emotionalism or fanaticism. He had sufficient discernment to understand what God was doing. He then began to use his spiritual gift as a part of the teaching/training process of disciplemaking, and he exhorted them "to remain faithful to the Lord with steadfast purpose." Immediately he moved to ground new believers in the Word, to establish them and strengthen the steadfastness of their commitment, and to build basics into their lives so that they would be disciples rather than mere believers. This was the first thing he did, patterned after the first efforts of the disciples after they began to win people to Christ (Acts 2:42).

BARNABAS' CHARACTER

After the description of Barnabas' work in Antioch, Luke gives an assessment of his character. "He was a good man, full of the Holy Spirit and full of faith" (Acts 11:24). He was not just a nice guy, but a good man. Moderns may tend to write off that phrase as a casual description, but in Scripture "good" is used very carefully. One of its uses is in Jesus' interview with the rich young ruler. He addressed Jesus as "Good Master." Jesus challenged him, saying, "no one is good but God alone. Why do you call me good?" (Mark 10:18). If God alone is good and the source of good yet Jesus seemed good to the rich young ruler, should that not, upon consideration, tell the youth something about Jesus? Was not Jesus reflecting something of God in His own character? Jesus encouraged the young man to think about Himself and what that would mean in terms of commitment to Him. Goodness is one of the reflections of godliness of character. Thus when Luke describes Barnabas as a good man, he means that Barnabas is a man who reflects the goodness of God, i.e., the holiness of God's nature and the Christlikeness of God's character. He is God's man.

This description of Barnabas is not surprising in light of the next statement made about him, that he was "full of the Holy Spirit." It was not just any spirit, but the *Holy* Spirit of God. "Holy" indicates the character of God. The Holy Spirit was not simply in his life, but Barnabas was "full of the Holy Spirit." The Holy Spirit, present in the life of every believer born into the family of God, manifested Himself in fullness in Barnabas. Just as He came upon the apostles at Pentecost, taking total control and making them fully His, so the Spirit had come upon Barnabas. He is under the full control of the Spirit. Barnabas may have received the infilling of the Spirit in Acts 4 where he is first introduced. He could well have been among that company praying when the Spirit came (Acts 4:31). In any event, at this point he is a man living under the Spirit's total control and at the same time reflecting God's holy character.

The third statement about Barnabas is that he was "full of faith" (Acts 11:24). This is not simply faith to believe on the Lord and be saved, nor faith to trust the Holy Spirit to come in sanctifying power, but a fullness of faith to trust God for whatever God wants to do in his life. The evidence for this appears in his willingness to trust God and to talk with Paul to ascertain whether his conversion was genuine. Barnabas placed his life not in Paul's hands but in God's hands. Further, before he went to Antioch he had heard something of events there, but he does not know what awaits him, whether he will be welcomed and how God will support him. Nonetheless, he was willing to trust God in these matters. And God was able to use Barnabas because he did have faith that led to obedience.

The Lord works to establish these three characteristics in every disciple. He purposes that His followers will get to the place where they let Him shape their character, have full control of their lives, and put them in circumstances where they must trust Him in a variety of ways. It is as though He says, "I want you to trust me for bigger and better things. Let me use you in ways you never thought possible. Become willing to trust me and do as I ask." Barnabas was willing, and God used him in powerful ways.

BARNABAS ADDS PAUL TO THE TEAM

As a result of Barnabas' labor in training others and building them up in the faith, a large company was added to the Lord (Acts 11:24). Then even more began to believe and growing numbers became established in the faith. The work of the Spirit in Antioch created a problem for Barnabas. With a sizeable number of converts he lacked enough mature Christians to disciple them. It is possible that some of those who first preached the gospel there, i.e, men from Cyprus and Cyrene, had remained to assist Barnabas in the work of training new believers. Even so, he does not have enough help to fulfill the second half of the Great Commission in Antioch. This problem would be delightful to have in any church.

Barnabas' solution to the problem was the biblical principle of multiplication. Accordingly, he traveled to Tarsus to find Paul. Apparently he does not know Paul's exact location in the Tarsus area so he must search for him. Since any journey of that sort is difficult, it is evident that Barnabas is going to some pains to secure the right assistance in discipling new believers. When he finds Paul, the latter realizes that Barnabas has been led by the Spirit to come seeking him. Certainly, Barnabas shares with Paul what God has been doing, what is happening in Antioch, who is responding and what need exists to disciple those who have believed in the Lord.

Luke reports that in Antioch "for a whole year they met with the church and taught a large company of people" (Acts 11:26). Their work was a training ministry of exhortation and encouragement to round out the process of disciplemaking. This was what Jesus had told the disciples to do, and since Barnabas had learned the lesson well, he followed the pattern set by the Eleven. Then Paul, working under Barnabas' direction, began to develop the same commitment to make disciples.

CHARACTER OF THE CHURCH IN ANTIOCH

It is not surprising that it was in Antioch that the believers were called Christians for the first time (Acts 11:26). The word was not just a label to identify followers of Christ. Rather, it indicated that they were beginning to reflect the character of Jesus. People noticed that they were like Him. It was not accidental that Barnabas, leading the team, was himself like the Lord, "a good man, full of the Holy Spirit."

When Barnabas reproduced himself, he raised up others who were also like Jesus. Every spiritual leader wants the Lord to do exactly the same. Disciples want to be like Jesus and then be given the privilege of reproducing themselves for God's glory.

In the last verses of Acts 11 appears an example of how Barnabas communicated one characteristic of his life to those whom he trained. The prophet Agabus came down from Jerusalem and warned the church by the Spirit that a great famine was near. The response at Antioch was revealing. "The disciples, each according to his ability, decided to provide help for the brothers living in Judea. This they did, sending their gift to the elders by Barnabas and Saul" (Acts 11:29–30).

This reaction is the opposite of much church policy today. Instead of Jerusalem believers, as the mother church, supporting Antioch, Antioch Christians wanted to help Jerusalem Christians. Where did they learn to give? From whom did they get the spirit of giving? They got it from Barnabas. One of the first things reported about Barnabas was that he gave freely of what he had (Acts 4:37). The sending of relief to Christians in Judea exemplified multiplication of that characteristic. The Christians at Antioch had made giving a regular part of their spiritual lifestyle, and they wanted to share, not only with fellow Christians at Antioch but also with the Christians in Jerusalem. They send the offering by the hands of Barnabas and Saul who then return, taking with them Barnabas' nephew John Mark (Acts 12:25). He joins them, perhaps living with Barnabas as they minister at Antioch.

MISSIONARY CALL TO LEADERSHIP
AT ANTIOCH

Barnabas and his team appear again in Acts 13, the opening of the last major section of the book. It is the part of Acts that focuses upon the great missionary thrust of the church. Among the leadership at Antioch are prophets and teachers, of whom the names of five are recorded (Acts 13:1). Barnabas and Saul have already been introduced, but three others served with them: Simeon, Lucius and Manaen. Where did these men come from? How did they get on the leadership team? While Luke is not explicit, the best hypothesis is that they became a part of the spiritual leadership team because Barnabas brought them on board just as he had brought Paul. Either he sought them out in another place and urged them to join the team, or he raised them up from within the church in Antioch.

In any event, Barnabas gathered around him a leadership team of four other men and invested his life in them as well. That group included both prophets and teachers. This means that they had a prophetic ministry of proclamation and evangelism, and a teaching ministry that involved building up, encouraging, and training believers. With their different gifts the team reflected a balance to fulfill both halves of the Great Commission.

While the leaders at Antioch were on a retreat, worshiping the Lord and fasting, the Holy Spirit spoke. "Set apart for me Barnabas and Saul for the work to which I have called them" (Acts 13:2). These men were not fanatics. They wanted to be sure that it was the Spirit speaking and not their own impulsiveness. So they continued to fast and pray to be certain that they had understood the Spirit's leading. When they were assured that they had the mind of the Lord, they laid their hands on Barnabas and Paul and sent them off. Confident that the Lord had spoken, they acted. They did not wait; they did not stall. They did not ask, "How are we going to do this?" They simply did what God asked them to do.

It is significant that the Spirit chose Barnabas and Paul, the two senior men of the church, to fulfill this assignment. The practice today is to keep senior men at home and to send off younger men for missionary service. Apparently on this occasion the Holy Spirit wanted His most seasoned disciplemakers out establishing churches. So He picked the older two men. Notice the implications of this choice. The selection of

Barnabas and Paul means that the work at Antioch was left in the hands of the three junior members of the team. Barnabas had invested himself so significantly in the three younger members that the Holy Spirit felt confident about their ability to lead the home church. The work of discipleship training had been done well enough that they could be left in charge of a growing congregation.

After the team was certain that they had understood the leading of the Lord, they commissioned Barnabas and Paul for their new task. The laying on of hands symbolically says, "You represent us. We believe in you. We are praying for you. We are committed to you. We want to help you in any way we can. We are with you in spirit and in all that God does through you." Also, in the laying on of hands, the three leaders participated personally and linked the entire congregation at Antioch with the mission of Barnabas and Paul.

The responsibility of the church for that missionary venture is only half the story. The other half comes into view with the phrase "being sent out by the Holy Spirit" (Acts 13:4). The Holy Spirit and the people of God together were responsible for this missionary thrust. Both were involved in the process. In this case the Holy Spirit supported them through the encouragement, prayers, and backing of the church in Antioch. It is another example of God's preferred pattern of ministry; He chooses to work through His people.

Barnabas and Paul went down to Seleucia and from there to Cyprus. When they arrived at Salamis, they continued their dual ministry. They declared the Word of God first in Jewish synagogues, i.e., proclamation, outreach, and evangelism. At the same time they had John Mark to assist them, indicating that while involved in proclamation and evangelism, they were also discipling a member of their own team. They continued to fulfill the two parts of the Great Commission as the norm for ministry.

FIRST MISSIONARY JOURNEY

This mission thrust from Antioch is usually referred to as the first missionary journey of Paul, but it really was the first missionary journey of Barnabas. Although Paul was vitally involved in what happened, he was still the junior member of the team. The people to whom they ministered were aware of this. At Lystra Paul healed a man who had been crippled from birth. In response the people said, "The gods have come down to us in the likeness of men! Barnabas they called Zeus, and Paul, because he was the chief speaker, they called Hermes" (Acts 14:11–12). Zeus, of course, was the chief god of the Greek pantheon. Thus in effect the men of Lystra said, "Barnabas is obviously the leader; he must be Zeus." Paul was the chief speaker and like Hermes, an orator. Yet Barnabas continued as team leader.

This event at Lystra also reveals something else significant about Barnabas as a disciplemaker. He recognized that in order to lead he did not always have to be the front man. Leaders should not do everything themselves. If others' gifts are stronger in certain areas, leaders must use them even if it means that leaders stand in the background. In fact, sometimes others may not be so gifted, but they need the experience and opportunity. This is a sign of a wise team leader, and Barnabas fit that category.

At the end of this pioneer journey, Barnabas and Paul return to spend some time with the disciples in Antioch (Acts 14:28). While there, the blessing of God on their ministry among Gentiles leads to the need for the great Jerusalem conference (Acts 15). Since Gentiles were responding to the gospel in significant numbers, the church had to work through the question of how gentile Christians were to relate to the Old Testament, particularly the Mosaic law. Barnabas and Paul went to Jerusalem to discuss this matter with the apostles and elders. After the conference agreed that Gentiles did not have to become Jews to be Christians, they returned to Antioch and continued their ministry. Luke reports, "Paul and Barnabas remained in Antioch, teaching and preaching the word of the Lord, with many others also" (Acts 15:33). The reference to "many others also" seems to imply that more than the original three were now on their ministry team (Acts

13:1). The leadership had multiplied in their absence, and others had been included to serve a growing and multiplying congregation. At the same time, Barnabas and Paul return to invest their lives in those in ministry at Antioch.

SEPARATION OF BARNABAS AND PAUL

The final verses of Acts 15 record the separation of the two men. The Spirit was apparently convinced that Paul's training was over and that he was now ready to lead his own team in the second phase of the missionary enterprise. The occasion of the separation rises during their planning of the second missionary tour. Paul disagreed with Barnabas over the application of one of the basic principles of discipleship, that of investing one's life in faithful Christians (cf. 2 Tim. 2:2). The fact that John Mark had withdrawn from them in the work at Pamphylia and returned to Jerusalem midway through the first missionary journey indicated to Paul that the young man was unfaithful. Paul knew that he had only so much time and energy to invest in a team, and he wanted that time to count for maximum effectiveness. So he insisted that they find a more dependable person to become part of the team. Barnabas apparently felt that John Mark's withdrawal was the result of his immaturity and that Mark's subsequent growth warranted a second chance. Over this difference of opinion Barnabas and Paul separated.

It is significant that the disagreement was not whether they should take someone with them to disciple on their journey. The question is one of whom to take. On this occasion Paul was right with regard to the principle of faithfulness, but Barnabas was correct about the man involved. It seems likely that the Holy Spirit used this difference of opinion to divide the disciplemaking team and thereby multiply the ministry sent out from Antioch.

PAUL'S MISSIONARY TEAM

Barnabas took John Mark and sailed off to Cyprus, while Paul chose Silas and journeyed through Asia Minor. Paul's team headed for his own home area. When they reached Derby and Lystra, Paul invited Timothy to join them; by the time they reached Troas, Luke had become a member of the group (Acts 16:8–10). From this point in Paul's ministry a team was always with him, surrounding, supporting, observing him. Whenever he taught they listened, learning how and what to teach. When he met with a group of elders, they watched so that they might learn how to lead. Whenever he was persecuted they saw how he coped with opposition. When he spoke before leaders, they noted his methods. They learned how to be abased and how to abound; how to be rewarded and encouraged; how to suffer triumphantly. They may well have served in numerous menial tasks such as buying ship tickets, packing the baggage, cooking food, washing clothes, and making tents. But in the process they are being trained to be men of God whom Paul can ultimately trust to serve God for His glory.

Later when Paul was confined to prison and could not travel, his ministry continued because he had multiplied himself. Thus he sent Titus to Crete, Timothy to Ephesus, Epaphroditus to Colossae, and others to a number of different places. His training had made them, in the best sense, extensions of himself. They represented him. A notable example was during his house arrest in Rome when he sent his team here and there. Because of the discipleship process that had taken place over the years, Paul was not limited to that location for ministry. It was, of course, the Lord's pattern.

The pattern is pertinent for us. Are we engaged in disciplemaking so that our ministries will continue through those whom we have trained regardless of age, infirmity, sickness, or whatever may limit our service?

BARNABAS' INFLUENCE

While Paul formed a team ministry of his own, Barnabas took John Mark and went to Cyprus, his native country. There they began to build up believers who had been won to

Christ on their previous visit. Not much is said about Barnabas subsequently. He is mentioned briefly by Paul in his letters to the Galatians and the Corinthians. The first letter to Corinth was not written until the latter part of Paul's ministry. There Paul refers to his own ministry and asked, "Is it only Barnabas and I who have no right to refrain from working for a living?" (1 Cor. 9:6). He continues to link himself to Barnabas in an affectionate way, even though years had passed since they worked as a team.

In following years little was written in the New Testament about Barnabas, but much is said about those in whom he invested his life, particularly John Mark. The author of the second Gospel keeps showing up in Scripture. At the end of Paul's letter to the church at Colossae (Col. 4:10) and his personal letter to Philemon (v. 24), he mentions that John Mark is a part of his team in Rome. In his last letter he writes to Timothy, "Get Mark and bring him with you; for he is very useful in serving me" (2 Tim. 4:11). Paul, in his wisdom and maturity, realized that John Mark's continued training under Barnabas readied him to serve in other capacities. So he welcomed the younger man to his own team. It says something about the largeness of Paul's spirit that he was willing to include someone discipled by Barnabas who he himself had concluded was not trainable. Paul continued to grow in his appreciation both of the way God works and of those whom He employs for His purposes.

Finally, at the end of his first epistle, Peter sends greetings from John Mark (1 Peter 5:13). One of the best early traditions is that the latter served as Peter's interpreter in Rome. For this reason, many scholars believe that Mark's Gospel reflects Peter's version of the story of Jesus. Because John Mark translated the gospel story over and over again for Peter, he had a sound basis for the data in his Gospel. Ultimately, John Mark became a significant leader in the early church, useful to God and effective chiefly because he had been discipled by Barnabas. It takes a person of Barnabas' discernment to recognize God's potential in someone like

John Mark, and a person of Barnabas' gifts to train the John Marks of the world for useful service to the Lord and the church.

The influence of Barnabas upon the entire church appears more clearly when we realize how much of the New Testament was written by men trained directly by Barnabas or by those whom he had discipled. John Mark and Paul were both trained directly by Barnabas while Luke was discipled by Paul. Those three alone wrote the second and third Gospels, the book of Acts, and all of Paul's letters. Thus a sizeable block of the New Testament was written by those directly or indirectly influenced by one man.

Yet in spite of this contribution, many Christians do not even know Barnabas' name. That would probably not bother Barnabas inasmuch as he was not interested in making a name for himself but in following Jesus and making disciples for Him. The application of his life story to our generation is obvious. We do not need a position, title, or name recognition to count significantly for the kingdom of God. If, like Barnabas, we are willing to multiply ourselves by investing our lives in a few key people over a period of years, God will use them for His purposes in the world. Jesus' strategy worked for Barnabas. It still works.

11

Discipleship in God's plan

There is a flow to the biblical principles of discipleship. Discipleship is designed to be a part of the accomplishment of God's purposes in the world. It is a means, not an end in itself. Its chief function is to draw men and women to God so that He might do with them as He pleases.

Since discipleship's primary purpose has to do with relating to God, it is not surprising that the nature of God determines its role. As the Bible unfolds the purposes and plans of God for His people, so the nature and character of God are also progressively revealed throughout history. Particularly in the unfolding drama of salvation history, God makes Himself known as a triune being: Father, Son, and Holy Spirit. In a unique sense, our grasp of discipleship principles is closely tied to our increasing understanding of the holy Trinity throughout Scripture. This should not surprise us. As God makes Himself known, His design for mankind also becomes clearer. At the same time He more crisply identifies His means for accomplishing His purposes. As a result, when we get to the climax of God's purposes through the person of Jesus Christ, we understand more clearly the design and implementation of the discipleship process. Accordingly, let us take a trinitarian overview of the biblical principles related to discipleship that we have observed.

DISCIPLESHIP AND GOD THE FATHER

God the Father reveals His purposes early in Scripture. Genesis 1 and 2 make it clear that God made men for fellowship with Himself, to reflect His holy character, and to serve Him. When sin entered the world (Gen. 3), the intimate fellowship between God and man was broken, and from that point on people no longer reflected the moral character of God as they were designed to do. Nor were they serving God as they should. God's solution to the problem of sin was to enter into a covenant relationship with individuals. The covenants with Noah, Abraham, Isaac, Jacob, Joseph, and their families reveal God's desire to restore intimate personal relationships with men and women. This background makes it possible to understand the offer of the covenant to Israel at Sinai as an agreement designed to strengthen God's relationship with each individual but also to the entire group as a people of God's own possession. He wants to know and be known by those whom He is making into His own likeness.

The unfolding story of God's work in the world shows that a permanent, ongoing relationship with God is possible only by redemption through His grace. He declares His people righteous by faith, and then He makes them righteous and frees them both physically and spiritually to be His own.

The experience of God's saving grace continues right on through the New Testament. Salvation in the person of Christ begins with repentance and faith and is expressed in terms of justification by faith and an experience of new birth into the family of God. The only way to be a part of the people of God and a disciple of Jesus is to begin at the point of salvation by grace through faith.

From the beginning God has clearly distinguished between the initial step of faith in Him and an ongoing commitment to follow Him in a developing relationship. The first step of faith in God is like that which led to the deliverance of Israel from Egypt. A deeper level of trust is involved when the redeemed committed themselves to the covenant at Sinai. Beginning faith is essential, but God looks for more. He is after a deeper level of trust in Him like that which is reflected in the relationship of children to a father.

In the New Testament the pattern reappears. Repenting of their sins and believing on Jesus is a clear, definite step that many took. But responding to a call to discipleship was a different decision that some made and others did not. Decisions of faith are not to be identified with becoming disciples of Jesus. The latter cannot happen without the former. But many trust Him for salvation who do not become His disciplined followers.

God has also made known from the earliest time His objectives for the people who are personally related to Him. We have already mentioned that the chief objective was cultivation of that personal relationship with God. Closely joined to that purpose are two other major objectives God has for His people. One is that they learn to serve Him. This is the ministry objective. The other is that they reflect His holiness. This is the character objective. His holiness is revealed in many ways, but His moral holiness is especially characterized by the traits of righteousness and love. These are to be the foundational elements in all conduct and attitudes as God's people relate to others.

Under the New Covenant God's purposes remain the same. God's people are, first of all, to continue to learn to cultivate their relationship with God. At the same time they are called to follow Jesus so that He might make them "fishers of men." In other words their call to discipleship involves a clear-cut commitment to be trained for ministry. But they are also called to develop a character like the character of Jesus. The holiness of God is expressed in heart and life by letting God's grace develop a character that looks like the character of Jesus. Again, the chief components of that character seem to be tied up with a commitment to righteous living and a loving heart.

If God's purposes under the Old and New Covenants remain the same, so do some of His means of accomplishing them. In due course we will see new elements that are added in the New Testament, but certain of the means remain constant. One of those is living under the authority of God as He has spoken in His Word. This was first settled at Sinai when God gave Israel the ten words (Ex. 20) and then began to write down His word in the law for His people (Ex. 24). The people of God became a people of the book of God. In the New Testament, Jesus' role as Teacher makes it clear that He expects His disciples to live under the authority of His own teaching as well as that which God had already spoken in the Old Testament (Matt. 7:28). When He gives them commands, He expects them to obey. Living under the authority of God and therefore paying close attention to the words God spoke is essential for any disciple.

God has also chosen to call people into fellowship with one another as well as to fellowship with Himself. Because we are made in the image of God, we are social beings. A social nature means that we have need for one another. Accordingly, God's design is that His people follow Him together. So in Genesis He calls individuals and their families to follow after Him. In Exodus He calls them to follow Him together as a nation. Under the New Covenant Jesus forms chosen disciples into a band of twelve. They learn the secret that they need one another if in fact they are to follow after God as He desires.

Another of God's means to accomplish His objectives is His plan that we shall live by faith. Abraham's faith made it possible for him to enter and live in a covenant relationship with God. A deeper level of faith at Sinai made it possible for Israel to commit herself to a covenant with Him. The disciples chose to trust God in a deeper way so that they were able to respond to Jesus' call to follow Him. Deeper levels of commitment that require deeper levels of trust follow initial faith. From those deeper choices to trust comes a habit of continuous living by faith that is worked out in day-to-day experience. The call to live by faith has been a part of God's plan from the beginning and it continues through Scripture and into the present.

DISCIPLESHIP AND GOD THE SON

While the purposes and many of the means of God the Father remain consistent throughout Scripture, new elements are added with the coming of Jesus in the New Testament. The incarnation of Jesus brought several things into sharper focus. One is our understanding of the character of a holy God. Jesus demonstrated that it is possible to work out God's holy nature in terms of righteous behavior and loving attitudes. In His life we see the concrete expression of God's character in relationship to other persons.

Since Jesus is fully man as well as fully God, we see also the other side of the picture—what mankind is to be like. Jesus reveals God, but He also reveals what man was created to be. When man is what he was created to be, there is no disparity between his character and God's character. So Jesus gives us not only the full picture of what God is like, but He gives us a full picture of what man ought to be like.

Jesus also models for His people how to serve God. Through His own ministry He demonstrates the kind of ministry He wants for His followers. He is concerned about what they do with their lives, and in concrete situations He trains them to serve God and touch other people's lives for Him.

The process of discipleship is introduced by Jesus as a vehicle for effectively accomplishing His purposes. Discipleship is connected with an even deeper relationship with God by means of the personal connection with Jesus. The person-to-person relationship that Jesus had with each disciple was a vivid expression of the kind of relationship God has always desired with every man and woman. The first purpose of discipleship, then, is to cultivate an intimate relationship with Jesus. Out of that closer relationship with Jesus, the Lord more effectively shaped the character of His disciples into His own likeness and trained them for His service.

Jesus expands the whole methodology of discipleship which had been only implicit under the Old Covenant (chiefly in the family and in close one-on-one relationships). The discipleship method is designed to build relationships, and accordingly has several key ingredients. One principle is the essentiality of life-to-life sharing. Jesus shared His own life with the disciples, and at the same time they learned to share their lives with one another. Relationships cannot be developed unless time is spent together so that people can know one another intimately. Out of that personal knowing, they learn character and service from one another.

The second essential principle of discipleship is the cultivation of habit patterns that make it possible to develop one's relationship with God. Learning to pray, study the Scriptures, memorize the Word, fast, and worship in community are all part of the process of developing tools for the ongoing cultivation of one's walk with God. Disciples of every age have found these spiritual disciplines or means of grace to be necessary for a growing relationship with the Lord.

The third essential principle of discipleship is accountability. The disciples learned to be responsible to Jesus for their conduct, attitudes, ministry, and relationships. They also learned to be accountable to one another so that they could help one another to be and do as God wanted. Accountability is required because, though we are saved by grace, we are still fallen creatures. We are engaged in spiritual warfare, and the Enemy of our souls lurks nearby to lure us back into sin. One of our more effective protective devices against the forces of evil and our greatest aid to our continuing walk with Jesus is our accountability to Jesus and to other disciples.

Since the discipleship method is tied to the disciples' personal relationship with Jesus, the Twelve learn as they are with Him. Jesus' method of teaching is twofold. Some of it is formal, straightforward teaching of principles the disciples must build into their lives. Another part is the informal teaching in everyday situations where Jesus applies principles of truth to concrete experience. Both of these are possible because of the personal attachment of the disciples to Jesus over a period of years.

One of the things Jesus gave His disciples was an understanding of how they would accomplish His purposes in the world. He revealed to them the needs of mankind and the impossibility of meeting them without His strategy. Then He set before them a plan for the multiplying of their lives in a few other people through discipling. He introduced the twofold principle of 1) ministry by concentrating on a few people for purposes of 2) multiplying their lives and reaching the world for God. Jesus also trained them for public ministry to a larger number of people. But as He trained them for public ministry He prepared them for a private, concentrated ministry of discipleship. While He made it clear that this could be done only with a few, because of the multiplication principle, ultimately the world would be touched for God.

Setting this vision before them, He gave them a life assignment to fulfill that vision. Thus at the end of a three-year process, He sent them out to make disciples. They were to engage in evangelism and outreach on the one hand, but at the same time they were to link that process with training and discipleship proper. Basically they were to accomplish in other people's lives what Jesus had in theirs. The goal was to make disciples of all nations for God.

DISCIPLESHIP AND GOD THE HOLY SPIRIT

The role of God the Holy Spirit completes the trinitarian picture. With the coming of Jesus the New Testament adds significant dimensions to both God's purposes and His plans for accomplishing them. With regard to the redemption of the world and the discipling of individuals, Jesus did new things, yet He did them in harmony with what God had been doing throughout the centuries. Following the death, Resurrection, and Ascension of Jesus, there comes with the day of Pentecost a larger revelation of the person and work of the Holy Spirit. The Holy Spirit had been at work in the world from the beginning of creation (Gen. 1:2). But from Pentecost onward our understanding of the way He works in individuals is more nearly complete.

Now we know that the Holy Spirit is the connection between us and God the Father and God the Son. Personal relationships between believers and God have a three-fold dimension to them. The Spirit continues to serve as the agent of the Godhead in individual lives, and He has a special role as believers' ongoing guide and director. The Holy Spirit replaces the supernatural dimension of Christ's personal presence with the disciples. Because He is not incarnate in human flesh as Jesus was, the Holy Spirit is not the human disciplemaker that Jesus was. Yet He does replace the supernatural part of Jesus' divine character by His spiritual presence in and with every disciple.

The New Testament also makes clear that the Holy Spirit had another role related to the Twelve. When Jesus came to the end of their training, He knew that they still had unmet needs. Those were highlighted for us in our study of John 13, when we saw that their transformation of character was not yet complete. They did not yet love as Jesus loved. Nor was their service for the Lord complete as evidenced by their unwillingness to wash one another's feet. They lacked power to love and power for service. They were doing both in a significant measure, but both were incomplete.

One of the major reasons for the Holy Spirit to come at Pentecost was to make up that deficiency. Jesus knew that His men were not able to reflect His character to the world. And they were far from prepared for their ministry assignment of making disciples of all nations. So after He tells them about their life assignment, He commands them to remain in Jerusalem until they have been filled with the Holy Spirit.

With the coming of the Spirit in His fullness at Pentecost, Jesus accomplished two major intentions in the disciples. First, He did something more fully to complete the process of making their character like His own. The fullness of the Spirit brought a purifying of their hearts from self-centeredness, an ability to love as God loves, and power to obey the Lord fully in every area of their lives. Second, the fullness of the Holy Spirit brought a power for ministry that the disciples had not known before. This is expressed in terms of outreach to non-Christians, but also in the training necessary if they are to raise up new believers to be disciples of Jesus (Acts 2). So the chief results of the coming of the Holy Spirit to the disciples were in terms of Christ-likeness and empowerment for service.

As soon as the disciples were filled with the Holy Spirit, they began to fulfill their life assignment of making disciples. Acts 2 gives a graphic picture of both outreach and initial discipleship. Throughout Acts we have seen that the disciples continued to invest in the lives of other people like Barnabas. The process persisted in the early church through leaders like Paul, Timothy, and others. The ongoing challenge to continue making disciples is encapsulated in 2 Timothy 2:2. Paul wrote to one whom he trained, "What you have heard from me before many witnesses entrust to faithful men who will be able to teach others also." These words remind us of Jesus' way of multiplying Himself. He invested in twelve disciples; some of them discipled Barnabas; Barnabas trained Paul; Paul discipled Timothy. Now Timothy is enjoined to do the same with "faithful men" who will be able to "teach others also." Thus discipleship goes on from life to life, from Jesus to the Twelve, to Barnabas, to Paul, to Timothy, to "faithful men," to "others," and on to our generation. This strategy of Jesus, supervised by the Holy Spirit, clearly is God's plan for changing the world.

Jesus Himself did not begin His own public discipling ministry until He was filled with the Holy Spirit at His baptism. He did not allow the Eleven to begin on their own without the fullness of the Spirit. And the Holy Spirit was the key in Barnabas' and Paul's lives that made them effective ministers and disciplemakers. The Holy Spirit continues the process of using key disciples to make other disciples, the ongoing process of glorifying God, but He uses those in particular who have come to know Him in His fullness.

What the Father began to do under the Old Covenant, the Son continued to do and amplify under the New. The

Holy Spirit came in full measure to complement and complete the process to make a trinitarian pattern for the making of disciples of all nations. May He continue to do it in our age for His glory!

BIBLIOGRAPhy

Arn, Win. *The Master's Plan for Making Disciples.* Pasadena, CA: Church Growth Press, 1980.

Bender, Harold S. *These Are My People: The Nature of the Church and Its Discipleship According to the New Testament.* Scottdale, PA: Herald Press, 1962.

Benjamin, Paul. *The Equipping Ministry.* Cincinnati, OH: Standard Publishing Co., 1978.

Best, Ernest. *Following Jesus: Discipleship in the Gospel of Mark.* Sheffield, Eng: Dept. of Biblical Studies, University Press, 1981.

Bonhoeffer, Dietrich. *The Cost of Discipleship.* London: SCM, 1959.

Bounds, E. M. *Power Through Prayer.* London: Marshall Brothers, 1912.

Bruce, A. B. *The Training of the Twelve.* Grand Rapids: Kregel, 1971.

Catchpole, David. "Discipleship, the Law, and Jesus of Nazareth." *Crux,* 11, no. 1 (1976): 8–16.

Chambers, Oswald. *Approved Unto God.* London: Distributors: Simkin Marshall, 1941.

Chandapilla, P. T. "How Jesus Trained the Twelve." *Evangelical Missions Quarterly,* 5, no. 4 (1969): 210–18.

Coleman, Robert. *The Master Plan of Discipleship.* Old Tappan, NJ: Revell, 1987.

_____. *The Master Plan of Evangelism.* Old Tappan, NJ: Revell, 1963.

Collins, Gary R. *How to be a People Helper.* Santa Ana, CA: Vision House, 1976.

Coppedge, Allan. "Holiness and Discipleship." *Wesleyan Theological Journal,* 15 (Fall 1980): 80–97.

Cosgrove, Francis. *Essentials of Discipleship*. Colorado Springs, CO: NavPress, 1980.

_____. *Essentials of New Life*. Colorado Springs, CO: NavPress, 1978.

Douglas, James Dixon. "Disciples." *The New Bible Dictionary*. London: InterVarsity 1962, 312–13.

Eims, Leroy. *Disciples in Action*. Colorado Springs, CO: NavPress, 1981.

_____. *The Lost Art of Disciplemaking*. Colorado Springs, CO: NavPress, 1978.

_____. *Winning Ways*. Wheaton, IL: Victor, 1974.

Foster, Richard. *Celebration of Discipline*. San Francisco: Harper, 1978.

Foster, Robert. *The Navigator*. Colorado Springs, CO: NavPress, 1983.

Franzmann, Martin H. "Studies in Discipleship," *Concordia Theological Monthly*, 31, nos. 10 & 11 (1960), 606–25, 670–89.

Hadidian, Allen. *Successful Discipling*. Chicago: Moody Press, 1979.

Halverson, Richard C. *How I Changed My Thinking About the Church*. Grand Rapids: Zondervan, 1972.

Hartman, Doug, and Doug Sutherland. *A Guidebook to Discipleship*. Irvine, CA: Harvest House, 1976.

Henrichsen, Walter. *Disciples Are Made, Not Born*. Wheaton, IL: Victor, 1974.

Hyde, Douglas. *Dedication and Leadership*. South Bend, IN: University of Notre Dame, 1964.

Kinlaw, Dennis. *Preaching in the Spirit*. Grand Rapids: Zondervan/Francis Asbury Press, 1985.

Kuhne, Gary. *The Dynamics of Discipleship Training*. Grand Rapids: Zondervan, 1977.

_____. *The Dynamics of Personal Follow-up*. Grand Rapids: Zondervan, 1976.

Lake, Charles C. *The Biblical Basis for Discipleship Development in the Local Church*. D.Min. Diss., Asbury Theological Seminary, 1981.

MacDonald, William. *True Discipleship*. Kansas City, KS: Walterick Publishers, 1962.

Mayhall, Carole. *From the Heart of a Woman: Basic Discipleship from a Woman's Viewpoint*. Colorado Springs, CO: NavPress, 1976.

Moore, Waylon B. *Multiplying Disciples: The New Testament Method for Church Growth*. Colorado Springs, CO: NavPress, 1981.

Morgan, G. Campbell. *The Great Physician*. Westwood, NJ: Revell, 1937.

Ortiz, Juan Carlos and Jamie Buckingham. *Call to Discipleship*. Plainfield, NJ: Logos; London: Good Reading, 1975.

_____. *Disciple*. Carol Stream, IL: Creation House, 1975.

Peacock, Heber F. "Discipleship in the Gospel of Mark." *Review and Exposition*, 75 (Fall 1978): 555–64.

Phillips, Keith W. *The Making of a Disciple*. Old Tappan, NJ: Revell, 1981.

Rengstrof, K. H. "Mathetes." *Theological Dictionary of the New Testament*, 4, ed. Gerhard Kittel, trans. Geoffrey W. Bromiley. Grand Rapids: Eerdmans, 1967, 415–61.

Rogers, Cleon. "The Great Commision." *Bibliotheca Sacra*, 130, no. 519 (1973): 258–67.

Sanders, J. Oswald. *Spiritual Leadership*. Chicago: Moody, 1967.

Segovia, Fernando F. *Discipleship in the New Testament*. Philadelphia: Fortress, 1985.

Skinner, Betty Lee. *Daws: The Story of Dawson Trotman, Founder of the Navigators*. Grand Rapids: Zondervan, 1974.

Trotman, Dawson. *Born to Reproduce*. Lincoln, NE: Back to the Bible, 1970.

Vincent, John James. *Disciple and Lord: The Historical and Theological Significance of Discipleship in the Synoptic Gospels*. Sheffield, Eng: Academy, 1976.

Voelkel, Jack. *Student Evangelism in a World of Revolution*. Grand Rapids: Zondervan, 1974.

Warr, Gene. *You Can Make Disciples*. Waco, TX: Word, 1978.

Watson, David. *Called and Committed: World-Changing Discipleship*. Wheaton, IL: Harold Shaw, 1982.

Wilkins, Michael J. *The Concept of Disciple in Matthew's Gospel as Reflected in the Use of the Term "Mathetes."* Leiden, NY: E. J. Brill, 1988.

Willard, Dallas. *The Spirit of the Disciplines*. San Francisco: Harper, 1988.

Wilson, Carl. *With Christ in the School of Disciple Building*. Grand Rapids: Zondervan, 1976.

index